KEY
C000071074

CONSTITUTIONAL AND ADMINISTRATIVE LAW

JOANNE SELLICK

HODDER
EDUCATION
AN HACHETTE UK COMPANY

Orders: please contact Bookpoint Ltd, 130 Milton Park, Abingdon, Oxon OX14 4SB. Telephone: (44) 01235 827720. Fax: (44) 01235 400454. Lines are open from 9.00 - 5.00, Monday to Saturday, with a 24 hour message answering service. You can also order through our website www.hoddereducation.co.uk

If you have any comments to make about this, or any of our other titles, please send them to educationenquiries@hodder.co.uk

British Library Cataloguing in Publication Data
A catalogue record for this title is available from the British Library

ISBN: 978 0 340 94705 0

First Edition Published 2007
Impression number   10 9 8 7 6 5 4 3
Year   2012 2011 2010 2009

Copyright © 2007 Joanne Sellick

Hachette UK's policy is to use papers that are natural, renewable and recyclable products and made from wood grown in sustainable forests. The logging and manufacturing processes are expected to conform to the environmental regulations of the country of origin.

Typeset by Transet Limited, Coventry.
Printed in Great Britain for Hodder Education, an Hachette UK Company, 338 Euston Road, London NW1 3BH by CPI Cox & Wyman, Reading, Berkshire.

CONTENTS

TABLE OF CASES   vii

PREFACE   xiii

**Chapter 1 THE SOURCES OF CONSTITUTIONAL
            LAW – STATUTE, COMMON LAW
            AND CONVENTIONS**

1.1   The relationship between statute and common law   2
1.2   Ordinary statutes and constitutional statutes   3
1.3   Conventions   5

**Chapter 2 FUNDAMENTAL CONSTITUTIONAL
            CONCEPTS**

2.1   The rule of law   10
2.2   The separation of powers   17

Chapter 3 THE SUPREMACY OF PARLIAMENT

3.1   Parliament as the supreme law making authority   20
3.2   Unlimited legislative power   21
3.3   Ruling on the validity of Parliament's enactments
      – the 'enrolled Act' rule   23
3.4   Implied repeal   27
3.5   Limitations   29

Chapter 4 PARLIAMENT

4.1   Electoral law   35
4.2   Parliamentary privilege   42

Chapter 5 CENTRAL GOVERNMENT

5.1	Conventions of ministerial responsibility	50
5.2	Royal Prerogative	53

Chapter 6 LAW OF THE EUROPEAN COMMUNITY

6.1	Preliminary Reference Procedure (Art 234/EC)	65
6.2	The supremacy of EC law	66
6.3	Direct effect	69
6.4	Indirect effect	72
6.5	State liability	73

Chapter 7 MEMBERSHIP OF THE EU AND PARLIAMENTARY SUPREMACY

7.1	The European Communities Act 1972	79
7.2	Section 2(4) European Communities Act 1972 and the courts	80
7.3	The retention of express repeal	87

Chapter 8 CIVIL LIBERTIES

8.1	Freedom of expression	90
8.2	Freedom of the person	96
8.3	Freedom of association and assembly	100

Chapter 9 HUMAN RIGHTS

9.1	The ECHR: examples of cases invoking substantive rights	107
9.2	Human Rights Act 1998	114

Chapter 10 JUDICIAL REVIEW JURISDICTION AND PROCEDURE

10.1	Procedure of application for judicial review	123
10.2	Definition of a 'public body'	124
10.3	Sufficient interest or standing (*locus standi*)	125
10.4	Attempts to completely exclude judicial review completely	128

Chapter 11 JUDICIAL REVIEW: THE GROUNDS

11.1 The GCHQ case – the three grounds 131
11.2 Illegality 132
11.3 Irrationality/unreasonableness 139
11.4 Procedural impropriety 142

Index **148**

TABLE OF CASES

A v Secretary of State for the Home Department [2004] UKHL 56, HL 9, 16
A v Secretary of State for the Home Department (No 2) [2005]
   UKHL 71; [2005] 3 WLR 1249...16, 109
A v UK [2002] All ER (D) 264 (Dec), ECHR...34, 45
ADT v UK (2000) 2 FLR 697 113
Agricultural, Horticultural and Forestry Industry Training Board v
   Aylesbury Mushrooms Ltd [1972] 1 WLR 190 142
Amministrazione delle Finanze dello Stato v Simmenthal SpA
   (Case 106/77) [1978] ECR 629..67
Anisminic v Foreign Compensation Commission
   [1969] 2 AC 147, HL 122, 128
Ashby v White (1703) 2 Ld Raym 938, HL 34, 36
Associated Provincial Picture Houses v Wednesbury
   Corporation [1948] 1 KB 223, CA 130, 131, 139, 141
Aston Cantlow and Wilmcote with Billesley Parochial
   Church Council v Wallbank [2003] UKHL 37, HL 119
Attorney General v BBC [1981] AC 303 114
Attorney General v de Keyser's Royal Hotel Ltd [1920] AC 508................49, 55
Attorney General v Fulham Corporation [1921] 1 Ch 440 ....130, 132
Attorney General v Guardian Newspapers Ltd (No 1) [1987]
   3 All ER 316, HL (Spycatcher Case)...89, 91
Attorney General v Guardian Newspapers Ltd (No 2) [1990]
   1 AC 109; [1988] 3 WLR 776 ....91, 114
Attorney General v Jonathan Cape Ltd [1976] QB 752, QBD 1, 5
Attorney General for Hong Kong v Ng Yuen Shiu [1983]
   2 AC 629, PC 130, 146
Attorney General for New South Wales v Trethowan and Others
   [1932] AC 526, PC 19, 29

BBC v Johns [1964] 1 All ER 923; [1965] Ch 32 ....54, 58
Barnard v National Dock Labour Board [1953] 2 QB 18 137

Beatty v Gillbanks (1882) 9 QBD 308, CA 89, 100

Bellinger v Bellinger [2003] 2 All ER 593 117

Benham v UK (1996) 22 EHRR 293 110

Bibby v Chief Constable of Essex (2000) *The Times,* 24 April 104

Billesley Parochial Church Council v Wallbank (2001) 106

Blackburn v Attorney General [1971] 1 WLR 1037; [1971]
   2 All ER 1380, CA 19, 32, 61, 78, 79

Bowles v Bank of England [1913] 1 Ch 57 27

Bradbury v Enfield London Borough Council [1967]
   1 WLR 1311, CA 130, 142

Bradlaugh v Gosset (1884) 12 QBD 271, QBD 34, 47

Brasserie du Pêcheur SA v Federal Republic of Germany
   (Cases C-46/93, C-48/93) [1996] ECR I-1029; joined with
   R v Secretary of State for Transport, ex parte Factortame Ltd
   (No 4) (Joined cases C-46/93 and C-48/93) [1996]
   2 WLR 506, ECJ 64, 74, 76

Breach v Freeson [1972] 1 QB 14 45

Brennan v UK (2001) *The Times,* 22 October 110

Bribery Commissioner v Ranasinghe [1965] AC 172 29

Brinkman Tabakfabriken GmbH v Skatteministeriet
   (Case C-319/96) [1998] ECR I-5255 76

British Oxygen Co v Board of Trade [1971] AC 610..............................130, 138

Brogan v UK (1988) 11 EHRR 117, ECHR....................................99, 106, 109

Bromley London Borough Council v Greater London
   Council [1983] 1 AC 768 ....130, 136

Bulmer v Bollinger [1974] Ch 401, HC 64, 65

Burmah Oil Company v Lord Advocate [1965] AC 75, HL..1, 2, 14, 19, 21, 55

CILFIT & I v Ministro della Sanita (Case 283/81) [1982] ECR 3415 66

Caballero v UK (2000) 30 EHRR 643 110

Cachia v Faluyi [2002] 1 All ER 192...117

Campbell v MGN Ltd [2004] UKHL 22 113

Campaign for Nuclear Disarmament v Prime Minister
   [2002] EWHC 2777 (Admin)..49, 62

Carltona Ltd v Works Commissioners [1943]
   2 All ER 560, CA 49, 50, 130, 137

Case of Proclamations (1611) 12 Co Rep 74; 77 ER 1352 ....19, 20, 49, 53

Case of Ship Money (R v Hampden) (1673) 3 St Tr 825 ....20, 49, 54

Case of the Sheriff of Middlesex (1840) 11 A & E 273 46

Chahal v UK (1997) 23 EHRR 413, ECHR 106, 108

Cheney v Conn [1968] 1 All ER 779, HC 19, 22

Christie v Leachinsky [1947] AC 573, HL 89, 96

Church of Scientology v Johnson Smith [1972] 1 QB 522 44

Congreve v Home Office [1976] QB 629 ....130, 135

Costa v ENEL [1964] (Case 6/64) [1964] ECR 1125, ECJ.......................64, 67

Council of Civil Service Unions v Minister of State for the
    Civil Service [1985] AC 374
    (GCHQ Case), HL 49, 59, 60, 131, 139, 143, 147

Critchel Down Affair (1953) Cmnd 9220 1954 HMSP 49, 51

Customs and Excise Commissioners v ApS Samex [1983] 3 All ER 1042........65

D v UK (1997) 24 EHRR 423 109

Day v Savadge (1615) 86 ER 235 24

De Freitas v Benny [1976] AC 239 60

Dean of Ely v Bliss (1842) 5 Beav 574 28

Defrenne v SABENA (Case 43/75) [1978] ECR 1365....................................69

Denkavit International BV v Bundesamt für Finanzen
    (Cases C-283, 291 and 292/94) [1996] ECR I-5063 76

Derbyshire County Council v Times Newspapers Ltd [1993] AC 534 114

Dillenkofer v Federal Republic of Germany [1996] ECR I-4845................64, 77

Dimes v Grand Junction Canal Co (1852) 3 HL Cas 759, HL.............130, 145

Director of Public Prosecutions v Jones [1999] 2 AC 240, HL 89, 100, 102

Director of Public Prosecutions v Luft [1977] AC 962 ....34, 38

Douglas v Hello! Ltd [2001] QB 967, CA 113

Dr Bonham's Case (1610) 8 Co Rep 114 ....19, 23

Dudgeon v UK (1982) 4 EHRR 149, ECHR 106, 112

Duke v GEC Reliance Systems Ltd [1988] 1 AC 618, HL 78, 82

Duncan v Jones [1936] 1 KB 218, DC...89, 102

Duncan Sandys' Case (1938) decision of Select Committee.......................34, 43

Duport Steels Ltd v Sirs [1980] 1 WLR 142, HL...9, 17

East African Asians v UK (1973) 3 EHRR 76..109

Edinburgh and Dalkleith Railway v Wauchope (1842)
    8 Cl & F 710, CA 19, 24

Edwards v UK (2002) *The Times*, 1 April 99

Ellen Street Estates Ltd v Minister of Health [1934] 1 KB 590, CA 19, 27

Entick v Carrington (1765) 19 St Tr 1029 ....9, 10

Ex parte Cannon Selwyn (1872) 36 JP 54...25

Faccini Dori v Recreb Srl (Case C-91/92) [1994] ECR I-3325 71
Flockhart v Robinson [1950] 2 KB 498 101
Foster v British Gas (Case 188/89) [1991] 2 AC 306..................................64, 71
Francome and Another v Mirror Group Newspapers Ltd and
    Others [1984] 2 All ER 408..16
Francovich and Bonifaci v Italy (Cases C-6, C-9/90)
    [1991] ECR I-5357, ECJ..64, 73
Garland v BREL [1982] ECR 359, HL 78, 81, 82, 85, 87
Ghaidan v Godin-Mendoza [2004] UKHL 30, HL................................106, 115
Goodwin v UK (1996) 22 EHRR 123 95
Gough v Local Sunday Newspapers (North) Ltd [2003]
    2 All ER 456, CA...34, 41
Gouriet v Union of Post Office Workers [1978] AC 435...................................18
Grieve v Douglas-Home [1965] SLT 186...34, 39

Halford v UK (1997) 24 EHRR 523, ECHR 106, 112
Harris v Minister of the Interior [1952] (2) SA 428 29
Harper v Secretary of State for the Home Department [1955] Ch 238, CA 35
Hirst v City Council for West Yorkshire (1986) 85 Cr App R 143, DC..89, 101
Hirst v UK (No 2) (2005) 16 BHRC 409, ECHR 34, 35
Hubbard v Pitt [1976] QB 142...102

International Transport Roth GmbH v Secretary of State for the
    Home Department [2002] EWCA Civ 158 119
Internationale Handelsgesellschaft MbH v EVST (Case 11/70)
    [1970] ECR 1125, ECJ 64, 68
Ireland v UK (1978) 2 EHRR 25, ECHR 106, 108

Jordan v Burgoyne [1963] 2 QB 744 100
Jordan v UK (2003) 37 EHRR 52 107

Kampelmann v Landschafttsverband Westfalenlippe and Others
    [1997] ECR I-6907 72
Knight v Nicholls [2004] 1 WLR 1653..41
Knuller v DPP [1973] AC 423 ....89, 95, 96
Köbler v Republic of Austria (Case C-224/01) [2004] 2 WLR 976.................75

L v UK (2004) *The Times,* 19 October 110
Laker Airways v Department of Trade [1977] QB 643, CA.......................56, 58

Lee v Bude and Torrington Junction Railway Company (1871)
LR 6 CP 576 25
Lewis v Chief Constable of South Wales [1991] 1 All ER 206..........................98
Litster v Forth Dry Dock Ltd [1990] 1 AC 546 83
Liversidge v Anderson [1942] AC 206, HL..8
Lustig-Prean and Beckett v UK (2000) 29 EHRR 548....................................112

M v Home Office [1994] 1 AC 377, HL 9, 15, 18
Macarthys v Smith [1979] 3 All ER 32, CA 78, 80–82, 85, 87
McCann, Farrell and Savage v UK (1995) 21 EHRR 97, ECHR 106, 107
McGonnell v UK (2000) 30 EHRR 289 110
Madzimbamuto v Lardner-Burke [1969] 1 AC 645, HL 1, 7, 19, 26, 31
Malone v UK (1984) 7 EHRR 14, ECHR......................................13, 106, 111
Manuel and Others v Attorney General [1983] 1 Ch 77, CA 1, 7, 19, 26, 32
Marleasing SA v La Commercial Internacional de
Alimentacion SA (Case 106/89) [1992] 1 CMLR 305.............................72, 82
Marshall v Southampton and South West Hampshire Area
Health Authority (No 1) (Case 152/84) [1986] QB 401, ECJ 64, 71
Mercury Communications plc v Customs and Excise
Commissioners [1997] 2 All ER 366..124
Merkur Island Shipping Corp v Laughton and Others [1983]
2 AC 570, HL 9, 12
Metropolitan Properties Co v Lannon [1969] 1 QB 577 145
Mortensen v Peters (1906) 14 SLT 227, HC 19, 22
Moss v McLachlan [1985] IRLR 76, DC...89, 103, 105
Murray v UK (1996) 22 EHRR 29 110

National Union of Teachers v Governing Body of St Mary's
Church of England (Aided) Junior School [1997] IRLR 242.......................71
Norbrook Laboratories Ltd v Minister of Agriculture, Fisheries and
Food (Case C-127/95) [1998] ECR I-1531 76
Observer, The and The Guardian v UK (1991) 14 EHRR 153.......................92
O'Hara v UK (2001) The Times, 13 November 110
Oldham v UK (2001) 31 EHRR 34 110
O'Loughlin v Chief Constable of Essex [1998] 1 WLR 374, CA 89, 98
O'Reilly v Mackman [1983] 2 AC 237, HL...122, 123
Osman v DPP (1998) 29 EHRR 245, ECHR...................................89, 98, 110

Parliamentary Election for Bristol South East, Re [1964] 2 QB 257 48

Pepper v Hart [1983] 2 WLR 1032, HL 34, 47
Perilly v Tower Hamlets Borough Council [1973] QB 9........................130, 133
Phillips v Eyre (1870) LR 6 QB 1 ....2, 9, 13
Pickin v BRB [1974] AC 765, HL 19, 25
Pickstone v Freemans plc [1989] AC 66 83
Piddington v Bates [1960] 3 All ER 660, DC 89, 102, 105
Poplar Housing and Regeneration Community Association Ltd v
   Donoghue [2001] EWCA Civ 595 120
Porter v Magill [2002] 2 AC 357; [2001] UKHL 673, HL............130, 135, 146
Prebble v Television New Zealand Ltd [1994] 3 All ER 407 47
Pretty v UK (2002) 35 EHRR 1 107
Price v UK (2001) *The Times,* 13 August 99
Prohibitions del Roy (Case of Prohibitions) (1607) 12 Co Rep 63 53
Pubblico Ministerio v Ratti (Case 148/78) [1979] ECR 1629 70
Pyx Granite Co Ltd v Minister of Housing and Local Government
   [1958] 1 QB 554, HL 130, 140

R v A (Complainant's Sexual History) (2001) *The Times,* 24 May, HL 106, 115
R v BBC, ex parte Referendum Party (1997) *The Times,* 29 April, DC......34, 39
R v Bentley [1998] TLR 31 July, CA 49, 60
R v Boundary Commission for England, *ex parte* Foot [1983]
   QB 600, HC 34, 36
R v Bow Street Magistrates' Court, *ex parte* Pinochet Urgart
   (No 2) [1999] 2 WLR 272, HL 130, 145
R v Broadcasting Complaints Commission, *ex parte* Owen
   [1985] QB 1153...40
R v Criminal Injuries Compensation Board, *ex parte* Lain [1967]
   2 QB 864 ....49, 58
R v Director of Public Prosecutions, *ex parte* Kebeline and Others [1999]
   3 WLR 175 117
R v Director of Public Prosecutions, *ex parte* Manning and Another [2000]
   3 WLR 463 145
R v Disciplinary Committee of the Jockey Club, *ex parte* Aga Khan [1993]
   1 WLR 909, CA 122, 124
R v Gibson [1990] 2 QB 619 96
R v HM Treasury, *ex parte* BT plc (Case C-392/93) [1996]
   ECR I-1631 ....64, 75
R v HM Treasury, *ex parte* Smedley [1985] QB 657; [1985]
   1 All ER 589 ....18, 126

R v Hillingdon London Borough Council, *ex parte* Royco Homes Ltd
    [1974] QB 720...140
R v Horseferry Road Magistrates' Court, ex parte Bennett [1994]
    AC 42, HL..8, 11
R v Howell [1982] QB 416..104
R v Hull University Visitor, *ex parte* Page [1993] AC 682 129
R v Inland Revenue Commissioners, *ex parte* National Federation of
    Self-employed and Small Businesses [1982] AC 617, HL 122, 125
R v Inland Revenue Commissioners, *ex parte* Rossminster Ltd [1980]
    AC 953, HL...9, 11
R v International Stock Exchange, *ex parte* Else [1993] QB 534 65
R v Jones (1999) 2 Cr App R 253...38
R v Lambert, Ali and Jordan [2001] 1 All ER 1014 117
R v Liverpool Crown Court, *ex parte* Luxury Leisure Ltd (1998)
    The Times, 26 October...136
R v Longman [1988] 1 WLR 619, CA...89, 96
R v Minister of Agriculture Fisheries and Food, *ex parte*
    Hamble Fisheries Ltd [1995] 2 All ER 714..147
R v Minister of Agriculture Fisheries and Food, *ex parte*
    Hedley Lomas (Ireland) Ltd [1996] ECR I-2553, ECJ 64, 76
R v Monopolies and Mergers Commission, *ex parte* South Yorkshire
    Transport Ltd [1993] 1 All ER 289...133
R v North and East Devon Health Authority, *ex parte* Coughlan
    [2001] QB 213...147
R v Panel on Takeovers and Mergers, *ex parte* Datafin [1987]
    QB 815, CA..122, 124
R v Poole Borough Council, *ex parte* BeeBee [1991] 2 PLR 27 127
R v Rule [1937] 2 KB 375, CA...34, 44
R v Secretary of State for Employment, *ex parte* Equal Opportunities
    Commission [1995] 1 AC 1 ....86, 128
R v Secretary of State for Foreign and Commonwealth Affairs, *ex parte*
    Council of Civil Service Unions [1984] IRLR 309 55
R v Secretary of State for Foreign and Commonwealth Affairs,
    ex parte Everett [1989] QB 811, CA 49, 62
R v Secretary of State for Foreign and Commonwealth Affairs,
    ex parte Rees-Mogg [1994] QB 552; [1994] 2 WLR 115, CA 49, 61, 80, 126
R v Secretary of State for Foreign and Commonwealth Affairs,
    ex parte World Development Movement [1995] 1 All ER 611 ..127, 130, 134

R v Secretary of State for the Environment, *ex parte* Greenpeace Ltd
(No 2) [1994] 4 All ER 352 ....122, 127

R v Secretary of State for the Environment, *ex parte* Rose Theatre Trust
Co Ltd [1990] 2 WLR 186 ....122, 126

R v Secretary of State for the Home Department,
ex parte Al Fayed [1997] 1 All ER 228 145

R v Secretary of State for the Home Department,
ex parte Bentley [1994] QB 349 60

R v Secretary of State for the Home Department,
ex parte Brind [1991] 1 AC 696, HL 89, 90, 114, 130, 140

R v Secretary of State for the Home Department,
ex parte Doody [1993] 3 WLR 154, HL 130, 144

R v Secretary of State for the Home Department,
ex parte Fire Brigades' Union and Others [1995] 2 WLR 1, CA 49, 56

R v Secretary of State for the Home Department,
ex parte Hosenball [1977] 1 WLR 766; [1977] 3 All ER 452 8

R v Secretary of State for the Home Department,
ex parte Khawaja [1984] AC 74 ....130, 134

R v Secretary of State for the Home Department,
ex parte Northumbria Police Authority [1989] QB 26, CA 49. 57

R v Secretary of State for the Home Department,
ex parte McWhirter (1969) *The Times,* 20 October 36, 80

R v Secretary of State for the Home Department,
ex parte Pierson [1998] AC 539, HL 9, 14

R v Secretary of State for the Home Department,
ex parte Simms [1999] 3 WLR 328 138

R v Secretary of State for the Home Department,
ex parte Thakrar [1974] QB 684, CA 23

R v Secretary of State for the Home Department,
ex parte Venables [1998] AC 407 ....130, 133

R v Secretary of State for Transport, *ex parte* Factortame Ltd and
Others (No 1) [1990] 2 AC 85, CA 68, 78, 84, 86

R v Secretary of State for Transport, *ex parte* Factortame Ltd and
Others (No 2) [1991] 1 AC 603, HL...................................68, 78, 84, 85, 86

R v Secretary of State for Transport, *ex parte* Factortame Ltd and
Others (No 5) [2000] 1 AC 524; (1998) *The Times,* 28 April 75, 86

R v Somerset County Council, *ex parte* Fewings [1995] 3 All ER 20..............134

R v Talbot Borough Council, *ex parte* Jones [1988] 2 All ER 207 137

R v Tronah Mines Ltd [1952] 1 All ER 697, CA..34, 37

R (on the application of ABCIER) v Secretary of State for Defence [2002]
EWCA Civ 473 141

R (on the application of Alconbury Developments Ltd) v Secretary of
State for the Environment, Transport and the Regions
and other cases [2001] UKHL 23, HL 106, 118, 141

R (on the application of Bibi) v Newham London Borough Council
(2001) *The Times,* 10 May...147

R (on the application of Carson) v Works and Pensions Secretary
[2005] UKHL 37 117

R (on the application of Daly) v Secretary of State for the
Home Department [2001] 2 AC 532, HL 130, 141

R (on the application of H) v London North and East Region
Mental Health Review Tribunal [2001] EWCA Civ 415, CA...........106, 119

R (on the application of Jackson) v Attorney General [2005]
4 All ER 1253, HL 19, 27, 30

R (on the application of Julian West) v Lloyd's of London [2004]
EWCA Civ 506, CA 122, 125

R (on the application of Laporte) v Gloucestershire Chief Constable
[2006] UKHL 55, HL..89, 104

R (on the application of Pretty) v DPP (2001) *The Times,* 5 December 107

R (on the application of Pro-Life Alliance) v BBC [2003]
UKHL 23, HL 34, 40, 41, 89, 92

Rechberger and Greindle v Austria (Case C-140/97) [1999]
ECR I-3499 76

Reference Re the Amendment of the Constitution of Canada (1982)
125 DLR (3rd) 1 ....1, 6, 7

Ridge v Baldwin [1964] AC 40, HL...130, 142, 143

Rivlin v Bilainkin [1953] 1 QB 485, HC 34, 42

Roche v UK (2005) *The Times,* 27 October 112

Rost v Edwards [1950] 2 WLR 1280 ....45, 46

Roy v Kensington Family Practitioner Committee [1992] 1 AC 624 123

Ruffle v Rogers [1982] 3 WLR 143...41

Sagnata Investments v Norwich Corporation [1971] 2 QB 614 ....130, 138

Saunders v UK (1997) 23 EHRR 313..110

Secretary of State for Defence v Guardian Newspapers Ltd
[1985] AC 339, HL..89, 94

Shaw v DPP [1962] AC 220 ....89, 95

Smith v UK (2000) 29 EHRR 493 113

Steel and Morris v UK (2005) 41 EHRR 403 110
Stockdale v Hansard (1839) 9 Ad & E 1, QBD..............................27, 34, 46, 47
Stourton v Stourton [1963] P 302, HC 42
Strauss and the London Electricity Board (1956) decision of
  Select Committee 34, 43
Sunday Times v UK (1979) 2 EHRR 245, ECHR 89, 93

T and V v UK (1999) *The Times,* 17 December, ECHR.......................106, 110
Taylor v Thames Valley Chief Constable [2004]
  EWCA Civ 858, CA 89, 97
Thoburn v Sunderland City Council [2002] 1 CMLR 50, CA....1, 3, 19, 33, 88
Tolstoy Miloslavsky v UK (1995) 20 EHRR 442...92
Tyrer v UK (1978) 2 EHRR 1 109

Van Duyn v Home Office (Case 41/74) [1975] 1 CMLR 1, ECJ..............64, 70
Van Gend en Loos v Nederlandse Tariefcommissie (Case 26/62)
  [1963] ECR 1, ECJ 64, 66, 69
Vauxhall Estates Ltd v Liverpool Corporation [1932] 1 KB 733 28
Venables v New Group Newspapers Ltd [2001] Fam 430 113
Von Colson and Kamann v Land Nordrhein-Westfalen (Case 14/83)
  [1984] ECR 1891, ECJ 64, 72

W and B (Children: Care Plan), Re (2002) *The Times,*
  15 March, HL 106, 116
Waddington v Miah [1974] 1 WLR 683 114
Walker v Unison [1995] SLT 1225..34, 39
Webb v EMO Air Cargo (UK) Ltd [1992] 4 All ER 929, HL 78, 83
Wheeler v Leicester City Council [1985] AC 1054...136
Wilson v First County Trust Ltd (No 2) [2003] UKHL 40; [2003]
  3 WLR 568, HL 47, 115, 118

X v Morgan Grampian Ltd [1991] 1 AC 1...15, 89, 94

YL v Birmingham City Council and Others [2007] UKHL 27, HL......106, 120

Z v UK (2002) 34 EHRR 245 99

PREFACE

The Key Cases series is designed to give a clear understanding of important cases. This is useful when studying a new topic and invaluable as a revision aid.

Each case is broken down into fact and law. In addition many cases are extended by the use of important extracts from the judgment or by comment or by highlighting problems. In some instances students are reminded that there is a link to other cases or material. If the link case is in another part of the same Key Cases book, the reference will be clearly shown. Some links will be to additional cases or materials that do not feature in the book.

To give a clear layout, symbols have been used at the start of each component of the case. The symbols are:

 Key Facts – These are the basic facts of the case.

 Key Law – This is the major principle of law in the case, the *ratio decidendi*.

 Key Judgment – This is an actual extract from a judgment made on the case.

 Key Comment – Influential or appropriate comments made on the case.

 Key Problem – Apparent inconsistencies or difficulties in the law.

 Key Link – This indicates other cases in the text which should be considered with this case.

The Key Link symbol alerts readers to links within the book and also to cases and other material especially statutory provisions which is not included.

At the start of each chapter there are mind maps highlighting the main cases and points of law. In addition, within most chapters, one or two of the most important cases are boxed to identify them and stress their importance.

Each Key Case book can be used in conjunction with the Key Facts book on the same subject. Equally they can be used as additional material to support any other textbook.

The law is stated as I believe it to be on 31 May 2007.

Joanne Sellick

CHAPTER 1

THE SOURCES OF CONSTITUTIONAL LAW –
Statute, Common Law and Conventions

The relationship between statute and common law

Burmah Oil v Lord Advocate (1965)
Statutes can be passed by Parliament that override principles of common law because Parliament is supreme (see Chapter 3)

↓

Ordinary statutes and constitutional statutes

Thoburn v Sunderland City Council (2002)
Development of the idea that there are two types of statute – ordinary statutes subject to implied repeal and constitutional statutes that may be expressly repealed

↓

Conventions – the non-legal nature of conventions

AG v Jonathan Cape Ltd (1976)

Reference Re the Amendment of the Constitution of Canada (1982)

Manuel v AG (1983)

Madzimbamuto v Lardner-Burke (1969)

Note: for the Royal Prerogative, see Chapter 5

1.1 The relationship between statute and common law

> **HL** *Burmah Oil v Lord Advocate*
> **[1965] AC 75 HL**
>
> In 1942, British forces destroyed the company's oil installations in Rangoon to prevent advancing Japanese forces from gaining control of them. The British Government made an *ex gratia* payment of £4 million to the company in compensation. The company sued the government for £31 million in compensation.
>
> The House of Lords held that compensation was payable by the Crown for the destruction of property caused by exercise of the royal prerogative in relation to war (see Chapter 5).
>
> The Government immediately introduced the War Damages Act 1965. This statute retrospectively nullified the effect of the decision. This case therefore clearly demonstrates the subordination of the judiciary to Parliament because of the doctrine of parliamentary supremacy – statute overrides common law and Parliament has such legislative competence it can legislate retrospectively (see Chapter 3).
>
> See *Phillips v Eyre* (1870) LR 6 QB 1 in Chapter 2 at **2.1**.

1.2 Ordinary statutes and constitutional statutes

CA *Thoburn v Sunderland City Council* [2002] 1 CMLR 50

The Weights and Measures Act 1985 authorised the use of both metric and imperial measures for the purposes of trade. Subsequent regulations made under s 2(2) of the European Communities Act 1972 prohibited the use of both and gave priority to the metric system. It was argued that the 1985 Act had impliedly repealed s 2(2) of the 1972 Act and should therefore take precedence (for Key Cases on implied repeal, see Chapter 3).

The court held that there was no inconsistency between the 1985 and 1972 Acts, so there was no need to discuss the doctrine of implied repeal. However, Laws LJ stated that there should be recognition of a hierarchy of statutes with there being two types – ordinary and constitutional statutes. A constitutional statute would affect the legal relationship between the individual and the State in some general, overarching manner or would enlarge or diminish the scope of fundamental constitutional rights. In his opinion, Laws LJ considered the following as examples of constitutional statutes: Magna Carta 1215, the Bill of Rights 1688, the Act of Union, the Reform Acts extending the franchise, the Human Rights Act 1998, the Scotland Act 1998, the Government of Wales Act 1998 and the European Communities Act 1972.

Constitutional statutes, according to Laws LJ, should not be subject to implied repeal because they protect the special status of constitutional rights. Instead, such statutes are subject only to express repeal.

Laws LJ

'We should recognise a hierarchy of Acts of Parliament: as it were "ordinary" statutes and "constitutional" statutes.'

'Ordinary statutes may be impliedly repealed. Constitutional statutes may not. For the repeal of a constitutional Act or the abrogation of a fundamental right to be effected by statutes, the court would apply this test: is it shown that the legislature's actual ... intention was to effect the repeal or abrogation? I think that this could only be met by express words in the later statute, or by words so specific that the inference of an actual determination to effect the result contended for was irresistible. The ordinary rule of implied repeal does not satisfy this test. Accordingly, it has no application to constitutional statutes.'

Traditionally, the UK's uncodified constitutional system has not recognised any distinction between different statutes – each is passed using the same process, so no Act of Parliament has any formal special status. In traditional constitutional terms, no Act can be entrenched in that all Acts are subject to implied repeal. However, the courts have for some time considered the European Communities Act 1972 as having a special legal status in that implied repeal does not apply to it (see Chapter 7). The passing of the significant Human Rights Act 1998 has opened up the debate as to whether other statutes are so constitutionally significant that they cannot be impliedly repealed. The comments of Laws LJ in this case support this conclusion; however, this is yet to be commented on by the House of Lords.

For Key Cases on parliamentary supremacy and implied repeal, see Chapter 3.

For Key Cases on the special legal status of the European Communities Act 1972, see Chapter 7.

1.3 Conventions

QBD *AG v Jonathan Cape Ltd*
  [1976] QB 752

 The executors of Richard Crossman's (a former Cabinet Minister's) estate wished to publish his diaries. The diaries included Cabinet discussions. Under the convention of collective ministerial responsibility, such matters are confidential and may not be revealed except when required under law or with the authority of the Cabinet Secretary. The Government sought an injunction on the basis that publication would be a breach of confidentiality.

 The court recognised the existence of the convention but since it was a non-legal rule the court could not enforce it *per se.*

 While the court concluded that publication of such information could be a breach of confidentiality, on the facts it concluded that the information was over 10 years old and therefore no longer confidential.

Reference Re the Amendment of the Constitution of Canada
(1982) 125 DLR (3rd) 1

As a means of achieving full patriation of the Canadian constitution from residual British control, the Canadian Federal Government made proposals altering the distribution of powers between the provincial legislatures. A number of the Provincial Governments objected, claiming that the proposals would breach convention that they had to both request and consent to such changes.

The majority found that consent was required under convention but that the convention itself could not be enforced by the court. In addition, convention could not crystallise into law unless put in statutory form.

Martland J and Others
'The conventional rules of the Constitution present one striking peculiarity. In contradiction to the laws of the Constitution, they are not enforced by the Courts.'

'This conflict between convention and law which prevents the Courts from enforcing conventions also prevents conventions from crystallizing into laws, unless it be by statutory adoption.'

Examples of where conventions have been incorporated into statute are the Statute of Westminster 1931 and the Parliament Act 1911.

CA *Manuel v AG* [1983] 1 Ch 77

The facts are based on the same background as *Reference Re the Amendment of the Constitution of Canada* (1982). Aboriginal chiefs argued that the convention had crystallised into law so that actual consent had to be established. They had not provided their consent to the Canada Act 1982, although it had been agreed to by a large majority of the provinces. Section 4 of the Statute of Westminster 1931 was relied on, which did not enact the convention but incorporated it in a modified form.

Conventions are non-legal rules and cannot limit parliamentary supremacy. Hence, any Act of Parliament in breach of convention would nevertheless be upheld by the courts. In addition, Section 4 of the Statute of Westminster 1931 did not require actual consent to be given, only that any Act passed expressly declared that consent had been given, which the Canada Act did.

HL *Madzimbamuto v Lardner-Burke* [1969] 1 AC 645

It was argued that the Southern Rhodesia Act 1965 had been passed in breach of the convention that the consent of the colony be first obtained.

The supremacy of Parliament was paramount and no court could declare an Act of Parliament to be invalid because it might breach a convention.

Lord Reid

'It is often said that it would be unconstitutional for the United Kingdom Parliament to do certain things … But that does not mean that it is beyond the power of Parliament to do such things.'

In *R v Secretary of State for Home Department, ex parte Hosenball* [1977] 1 WLR 766; [1977] 3 All ER 452 a US citizen was to be deported on the basis that he was a threat to national security. The court used the existence of the convention to influence its decision. The court relaxed the usual rules of the law of natural justice justifying its decision by relying on the convention that the minister would have to be responsible to Parliament for his actions. See also *Liversidge v Anderson* [1942] AC 206 HL.

For Key Cases on parliamentary supremacy, see Chapter 3. For Key Cases on the rules of natural justice, see Chapter 11.

CHAPTER 2

FUNDAMENTAL CONSTITUTIONAL CONCEPTS

The Rule of Law

***Entick v Carrington* (1765)**
No-one may be punished in goods or person unless there has been a distinct breach of the law; officials must act within the constraints of the law

***R v IRC, ex parte Rossminster Ltd* (1980)**
Action taken within the authority prescribed by statute is lawful

***R v Horseferry Road Magistrates' Court, ex parte Bennett* (1994)**
Officials had abused their power resulting in the entire prosecution being unlawful

***Merkur Island Shipping Corporation v Laughton and Others* (1983)**
Laws should be clear

***Phillips v Eyre* (1870) and *R v Secretary of State for the Home Department, ex parte Pierson* (1998)**
Laws should not be retrospective

***M v Home Office* (1994)**
Government officials are subject to the law and the courts

***A v Home Secretary* (2004)**
Challenge to executive power to detain terrorist suspects

CONSTITUTIONAL DOCTRINES

The Separation of Powers

***Duport Steels Ltd v Sirs* (1980)**
The legislature makes the laws; the judiciary interprets them

***M v Home Office* (1994)**
The judiciary acts under the rule of law to check executive action

2.1   The rule of law

Entick v Carrington (1765) 19 St Tr 1029

 Two King's messengers, with a warrant issued by the Secretary of State, broke into Entick's house and took away papers. It was alleged that he was writing seditious material. Entick sued for trespass to his property and goods; the Government argued that the warrant was legal.

 There was no law supporting the issuing of the warrant and therefore it was illegal and void.

 Lord Camden CJ
'No man can set foot upon my ground without my licence, but he is liable to an action ... If he admits the fact, he is bound to show by way of justification, that some positive law has empowered or excused him.'

 Government according to the law means that neither the Executive nor any government official can exercise a power unless it is authorised by some specific rule of law. Dicey placed great emphasis on this case when explaining his meaning of the rule of law, namely that no person be punishable in goods or person except for a distinct breach of the law and that every person, irrespective of rank, be subject to the ordinary law of the land. It is Dicey's explanation of the rule of law that underpins traditional understanding of this constitutional doctrine.

HL   *R v Inland Revenue Commissioners, ex parte Rossminster Ltd*
[1980] AC 952

Officers of the Inland Revenue obtained warrants to search Rossminster's premises. The warrant did not clearly specify the tax fraud suspected.

The Court of Appeal ordered a grant of *certiorari* to quash the warrants because they did not specify the alleged offence. On appeal, the House of Lords concluded that the warrant had complied with the relevant statute (Taxes Management Act 1979) and was therefore valid.

The House of Lords took a restrictive approach: the warrant had complied with the wording of the statute and was therefore legal. However, their Lordships did express dismay that the Act granted such extensive powers.

HL   *R v Horseferry Road Magistrates' Court, ex parte Bennett*
[1994] AC 42

Bennett, a New Zealand citizen, was wanted by the police for alleged offences. He was arrested in South Africa. Even though there was no extradition treaty between the UK and South Africa, the police put him on a plane for the UK, where he was arrested. He was committed to the Crown Court for trial and challenged this decision. The Divisional Court dismissed the application on the basis that even if he had been illegally abducted his trial would still be fair.

The House of Lords reversed the decision. Bennett had been abducted in that he had been bought back to the UK in breach of the existing extradition process, international law and the laws of South Africa. The authorities had therefore abused their power and this resulted in the entire prosecution being illegal.

Lord Griffiths

' … the judiciary accept a responsibility for the maintenance of the rule of law that embraces a willingness to oversee executive action and to refuse to countenance behaviour that threatens either basic human rights or the rule of law'.

 HL *Merkur Island Shipping Corporation v Laughton and Others* [1983] 2 AC 570

Members of a Trade Union were sued for damages for losses arising from industrial action. The court was required to construe three statutes to identify whether, as a Trade Union, they were immune from tortuous liability.

The court expressed concern that it was required to spend considerable time interpreting three statutes that were not clearly expressed.

Lord Diplock

'Absence of clarity is destructive of the rule of law; it is unfair to those who wish to preserve the rule of law; it encourages those who wish to undermine it.'

One of the aspects of the rule of law is that laws should attain certain minimum standards. This includes that laws be clear, not ambiguous, vague or obscure.

See also *Malone v UK* (1984) 7 EHRR 14 in Chapter 9 at **9.1.5**.

Phillips v Eyre (1870) LR 6 QB 1

After the suppression of a rebellion, the legislature in Jamaica passed an Act which, if valid, would prevent the claimant from suing for assault and false imprisonment.

A court would not give retrospective effect to new legislation unless the legislature clearly intended this to be the case.

Willes J

' … the court will not ascribe retrospective force to new laws affecting rights, unless by express words or necessary implication it appears that such was the intention of the legislature'.

Another aspect of the rule of law in terms of the minimum standards that laws should meet is that they should generally be prospective and not retrospective. Hence, if a law is to be retrospectively applied it must either expressly state so or be clearly implied.

It should though be noted that Parliament, as the supreme legislative body, is able to pass retrospective laws; see *Burmah Oil v Lord Advocate* [1965] AC 75 and Chapter 1 at **1.1**. There is one qualification to this in that under Article 7 of the European Convention on Human Rights, retrospective criminal legislation is prohibited (see Chapter 9).

 R v Secretary of State for the Home Department, ex parte Pierson [1998] AC 539

In 1985 Pierson was convicted of murder and received two mandatory life sentences. The tariff (minimum period to be served) recommended by the trial judge and Lord Chief Justice was 15 years. The Home Secretary set the tariff at 20 years, on the basis that it was a double, premeditated murder. In 1994 the Home Secretary accepted that the murders were part of a single, unpremeditated incident but that 20 years was still appropriate. Pierson challenged this by judicial review.

Parliament had not conferred any general power on the Home Secretary to increase tariffs retrospectively and therefore he had acted unlawfully in increasing the tariff.

Lord Steyn
'The rule of law in its widest sense has procedural and substantive effect … Unless there is the clearest provision to the contrary, Parliament must be presumed not to legislate contrary to the rule of law.'

The potential for conflict between the rule of law and the supremacy of Parliament (see Chapter 3) is difficult to resolve. The relationship between the two doctrines was expressed by Lord Bridge in *X v Morgan Grampian Ltd* [1991] AC 1 (see Chapter 8 at **8.1.2**) who stated: 'The maintenance of the rule of law is in every way as important in a free society as the democratic franchise. In our society the rule of law rests upon twin foundations: the sovereignty of ... Parliament in making the law and the sovereignty of the ... courts in interpreting and applying the law.'

HL | *M v Home Office* **[1994] 1 AC 377**

M sought political asylum but his application was rejected by the Home Secretary. An injunction was issued but M was deported. The House of Lords considered whether a government minister or department could be found to be in contempt of court and whether an injunction could be enforced against them.

The Home Secretary had committed contempt of court by disobeying the injunction. In addition, there was power to grant injunctions against Ministers acting in their official capacity.

Dicey's explanation of the rule of law included, as his second proposition, the idea that every man was subject to the ordinary law and the courts. This case is an example of the courts applying this principle, one of equality, to a government minister.

The principle was also expressed by Lord Donaldson in *Francome and Another v Mirror Group Newspapers Ltd and Others* [1984] 2 All ER 408: 'Parliamentary democracy is … based on the rule of law. That requires all citizens to obey the law … There are no privileged classes to whom it does not apply.'

HL *A v Secretary of State for the Home Department*
[2004] UKHL 56

The power to detain foreign terrorism suspects under the Anti-Terrorism, Crime and Security Act 2001 was challenged under the Human Rights Act 1998.

The law infringed the ECHR and could not be exercised in such a way as to detain indefinitely without charge or trial.

Lord Nicholls
Imprisonment of such a nature would be an 'anathema in any country which observes the rule of law'.

There has been much criticism of the policies and legislation adopted to deal with the 'war against terrorism'. Generally, executive assessment of what should be considered a 'time of emergency' will rarely, if ever, be successfully challenged in the courts. This case is significant in that it shows a clear example of the rule of law operating to check the executive and protect the individual, enhanced by the passing of the Human Rights Act 1998. Similarly, in *A v Secretary of State for the Home Department (No 2)* [2005] UKHL 71 the House of Lords concluded that evidence that may have been obtained by torture in another country was not admissible.

For Key Cases on the Human Rights Act 1998, see Chapter 9 at **9.2**.

2.2 The separation of powers

HL *Duport Steels Ltd v Sirs* [1980] 1 WLR 142

Section 13(1) of the Trade Union and Labour Relations Act 1964 granted immunity to acts done 'in ... furtherance of a trade dispute'. This had to be interpreted in respect of strike action aimed at third parties.

The separation of powers underpins the constitution in that the judiciary only has the authority to interpret the law, as made by Parliament.

Lord Diplock
'It cannot be too strongly emphasised that the British constitution ... is firmly based upon the separation of powers; Parliament makes the laws, the judiciary interpret them.'

While there are numerous examples of fusion within the

British constitution, this case provides recognition of adherence to the doctrine in the context of the legislature and judiciary.

In *R v HM Treasury, ex parte Smedley* [1985] 1 All ER 589 Sir John Donaldson MR echoed the comments of Lord Diplock when he stated that 'it is a constitutional convention of the highest importance that the legislature and the judicature are separate and independent of one another'.

 M v Home Office [1994] 1 AC 377

See above.

Nolan LJ
'The proper constitutional relationship of the executive with the courts is that the courts will respect all acts of the executive within its lawful province, and that the executive will respect all decisions of the courts as to what its lawful province is.'

It is essential that the executive and judiciary are separate and that the latter has independence. This ensures that the rule of law can operate to check executive action, the relationship described above.

Gouriet v Union of Post Office Workers [1978] AC 435

CHAPTER 3

THE SUPREMACY OF PARLIAMENT

The principles of parliamentary supremacy

- Parliament is the supreme law-making authority
The Case of Proclamations (1611)

- Parliament has unlimited legislative authority
Burmah Oil Company v Lord Advocate (1965)
Mortensen v Peters (1906)
Cheney v Conn (1968)

- No court can question the validity of an Act – 'enrolled Act' rule
Dr Bonham's Case (1610)
Edinburgh and Dalkeith Railway v Wauchope (1842)
Pickin v BRB (1974)
Manuel and Others v Attorney-General (1983)

- No Parliament can bind a future Parliament – implied repeal
Ellen Street Estates Ltd v Minister of Health (1934)

Some limitations to parliamentary supremacy

- Manner and form argument
AG for New South Wales v Trethowan and Others (1932); *R (Jackson) v Attorney-General* (2005)

- 'Practical' limitations (validity vs effectiveness argument)
Madzimbamuto v Lardner-Burke (1969); *Blackburn v AG* (1971)

- Constitutional statutes
Thoburn v Sunderland City Council (2002)

3.1 Parliament as the supreme law-making authority

The Case of Proclamations (1611) 12 Co Rep 74; 77 ER 1352

The King sought to declare law through issuing proclamations. The Commons complained that this was an abuse of power. The King sought the opinion of Chief Justice Coke.

The monarch does not have the power to create law by proclamation.

Chief Justice Coke
' ... the law of England is divided into three parts, common law, statute law and custom; but the King's proclamation is none of them'.

This is one of a series of cases in the seventeenth century stemming from the battle between Parliament and the Stuart monarchs for supremacy. Their claims to rule by prerogative powers were resolved by the Bill of Rights 1688, under which Parliament became the supreme law-making authority. The following case provides another example of this.

Case of Ship Money (R v Hampden) (1637) 3 St Tr 825

Hampden refused to pay a tax levied by Charles I. The Crown argued that the monarch had prerogative power to raise taxes in a time of emergency.

The court upheld the power of the Crown.

The decision was reversed with the passing of the Shipmoney Act 1640 and the monarch's prerogative to levy taxes without Parliament's consent was made illegal under the Bill of Rights 1688.

For the Royal Prerogative, see Chapter 5 at **5.2**.

3.2 Unlimited legislative power

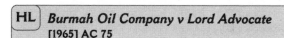

HL | *Burmah Oil Company v Lord Advocate*
[1965] AC 75

 See Chapter 1 at **1.1**.

 The company was successful.

 While the company was successful, Parliament immediately passed the War Damages Act 1965. This had retrospective effect – an example of the unlimited legislative power of Parliament.

Mortensen v Peters (1906) 14 SLT 227

Mortensen was the captain of a Norwegian trawler charged with illegal fishing under a byelaw. Statute stated that such byelaws could be applied to the area (the Moray Firth) even though much of it was international waters.

Parliament can expressly legislate for matters that are governed by international law and the courts will uphold such a statute.

Lord Dunedin
'For us an Act of Parliament duly passed by Lords and Commons and assented to by the King is supreme and we are bound to give effect to its terms.'

 Cheney v Conn [1968] 1 All ER 779

A taxpayer challenged his income tax assessment made under the Finance Act 1964 on the basis that some of the money would be used to finance the manufacture of nuclear weapons contrary to the Geneva Convention.

International law cannot place any limitations on Parliament's power.

Ungoed-Thomas J

'What the statute itself enacts cannot be unlawful, because what the statute says and provides is itself the law, and the highest form of law that is known to this country.'

 R v Secretary for the Home Department, ex parte Thakrar [1974] QB 684

The applicant claimed the right to enter the UK on the basis of a customary rule of international law.

No such rule of international law, even if it did exist, could prevail against any relevant statute, in this case the Immigration Act 1971.

3.3 Ruling on the validity of Parliament's enactments – the 'enrolled Act' rule

Dr Bonham's Case (1610) 8 Co Rep 114

This case considered whether there were moral limits to the scope of parliamentary power that could be enforced by the judiciary.

The judiciary were able to enforce moral and other limitations on the power of Parliament.

Chief Justice Coke

' … when an Act of Parliament is against common right and reason or repugnant, or impossible to be performed, the common law will control it, and adjudge such an Act to be void'.

This case precedes the Glorious Revolution of 1688 and the development of the doctrine of parliamentary supremacy and is hence no longer good law.

See also *Day v Savadge* (1615) 86 ER 235 where it was concluded that 'even an Act of Parliament, made against natural equity … is void in itself'.

CA *Edinburgh and Dalkeith Railway v Wauchope*
(1842) 8 Cl & F 710

Wauchope challenged an Act on the basis that he had not been notified of the Bill's introduction as required by standing orders of the House of Commons.

The court rejected the challenge.

Lord Campbell

'All that a court of justice can do is to look to the Parliament roll; if from that it should appear that a Bill has passed both

Houses and received the Royal Assent, no court of justice can inquire into the mode in which it was introduced into Parliament, or into what was done previous to its introduction, or what passed in Parliament during its progress in its various stages through both Houses.'

With the development of the doctrine of parliamentary supremacy, the courts no longer have any jurisdiction to question the validity of legislation, hence the function of the court is only to construe and apply Acts of Parliament.

In *Lee v Bude and Torrington Junction Railway Company* (1871) LR 6 CP 576 it was stated that 'if an Act of Parliament has been obtained improperly, it is for the legislature to correct it by repealing it; but so long as it exists as law, the courts are bound to apply it'. Similarly, in *Ex parte Cannon Selwyn* (1872) 36 JP 54 on the validity of the Irish Church Act 1869, Cockburn CJ stated that there was no body that could question the validity of an Act on the basis that legislation 'is superior in authority to any court of law'. The principle, known as the enrolled act rule, was reaffirmed in the following case.

HL	*Pickin v BRB*
	[1974] AC 765

Pickin argued that he had been deprived of an interest in land by the British Railways Act 1968. He claimed that the Act was invalid because it had been passed fraudulently.

The 'enrolled Act' rule, developed as part of the doctrine of the supremacy of Parliament, precludes the courts from investigating whether internal procedures of the House have been complied with; no court can question the validity of an Act of Parliament or disregard it.

 Lord Reid
'In earlier times many learned lawyers seem to have believed that an Act of Parliament could be disregarded in so far as it was contrary to the law ... but since the supremacy of Parliament was finally demonstrated by the Revolution of 1688 any such idea has become obsolete.'

Hence, all that a court can do is to 'construe and apply the enactments of Parliament'.

  See also *Madzimbamuto v Lardner-Burke* [1969] 1 AC 645 at **3.5.2**.

CA *Manuel v Attorney-General* [1983] Ch 77

See Chapter 1 at **1.3**.

It was held that the doctrine of parliamentary legislative supremacy applied and the Act therefore extended to Canada.

Sir Robert Megarry VC
' ... once an instrument is recognised as being an Act of Parliament, no English court can refuse to obey or question its validity'.

Once the court is satisfied that a document is an Act of Parliament, it will give it obedience. However, this does not extend to measures that fall short of being an Act. In *Stockdale v Hansard* (1839) 9 Ad & E 1 it was held that a resolution of the House of Commons had no legal force and that to have such force it had to be placed on a statutory basis.

Bowles v Bank of England [1913] 1 Ch 57.

See also *R (Jackson) v Attorney-General* [2005] 4 All ER 1253 at **3.5.1**.

3.4 Implied repeal

CA *Ellen Street Estates Ltd v Minister of Health*
[1934] 1 KB 590

The plaintiffs argued that an Act passed in 1919 providing higher levels of compensation for compulsory purchase should prevail over the levels provided for in a 1925 Act.

The implied repeal doctrine required that where a later statute was inconsistent with an earlier statute it impliedly repealed the earlier statute to the extent of the inconsistency.

Maugham LJ
' The legislature cannot ... bind itself as to the form of subsequent legislation, and it is impossible for Parliament to enact that in a subsequent statute dealing with the same subject matter there

can be no implied repeal. If in a subsequent Act Parliament chooses to make it plain that the earlier statute is being to some extent repealed, effect must be given to that intention just because it is the will of Parliament.'

This is an often cited authority for the traditional notion of parliamentary supremacy as explained by Dicey – that no Parliament has the authority to bind another Parliament; there can be no entrenchment. This is effective through the doctrine of implied repeal, which was described in *Dean of Ely v Bliss* (1842) 5 Beav 574 by Lord Langdale in the following terms:

'If two inconsistent Acts be passed at different times, the last must be obeyed, and if obedience cannot be observed without derogating from the first, it is the first which must give way ... Every Act is made either for the purpose of making a change in the law, or for the purpose of better declaring the law, and its operation is not to be impeded by the mere fact that it is inconsistent with some previous enactment.'

However, while the implied repeal doctrine still applies to most statutes, some senior judges regard it as inapplicable to statutes of major constitutional significance (see **3.5.3** and Chapter 1), such as the European Communities Act 1972 (see Chapter 7) and the Human Rights Act 1998 (see Chapter 9).

Vauxhall Estates Ltd v Liverpool Corporation [1932] 1 KB 733.

3.5 Limitations

3.5.1 Manner and form argument

 AG for New South Wales v Trethowan and Others
[1932] AC 526

Under the Colonial Laws Validity Act 1865, the New South
Wales legislature had the power to legislate for its own
constitution, provided the laws passed were in the 'manner
and form' required by colonial law. Under the Constitution
Act 1902, no Bill abolishing the Legislative Council could be
passed without a referendum and no Bill to alter this
requirement could be approved without a referendum. In
1930 two Bills were passed; one repealing the requirement for
a referendum prior to abolishing the Legislative Council and
the other abolishing the institution itself. The plaintiffs sought
injunctions preventing the presentation of both Bills for
Assent on the basis that they needed to be approved by a
referendum.

The court would grant an injunction to prevent a Bill being
submitted for Royal Assent if it did not comply with an
entrenched procedure.

This case is often cited in support of the argument that one
Parliament can place a binding manner and form requirement
on another. Support for this view can be found in *Harris v
Minister of the Interior* [1952] (2) SA 428 and *Bribery
Commissioner v Ranasinghe* [1965] AC 172. However,
opponents of this view believe that these cases can be
explained on the basis that the legislatures in these countries

were not truly supreme in the same way as the UK Parliament; the powers of the legislatures were established by a UK Act and therefore they were subordinate legislatures to the UK Parliament.

HL *R (Jackson) v Attorney-General* [2005] 4 All ER 1253

The Hunting Act 2004 had been passed under the Parliament Acts 1911 and 1949. It was argued that the 1949 Act was invalid on the basis that since it was passed under the 1911 Act it was delegated legislation and as such could not extend the powers of the Commons and that the 1911 Act implied that its procedure could not be used to further reduce the power of the Lords.

The 1949 Act was lawful since Acts passed under the 1911 Act's procedure were not delegated legislation and there was nothing within its terms that prevented it from being used to reduce the powers of the Lords. Since the 1949 Act was valid, the Hunting Act 2004 was also.

It appears therefore that the Parliament Acts could technically be used to achieve major constitutional change without the consent of the House of Lords. Whether this includes abolishing the Lords itself did not arise for decision. On extending the life of Parliament, expressly stated within the 1911 Act to require the consent of the House of Lords, a majority of nine held in *obiter* that the Parliament Act procedure could not be used to remove it. However, invoking the 1949 Act to make major constitutional changes was expressly doubted by Lord Steyn, implying that the courts have a role in ascertaining whether its use is constitutionally 'proper'. In addition, using the Act in such a way would probably raise considerable political criticism.

3.5.2 'Practical' limitations

PC *Madzimbamuto v Lardner-Burke* [1969] 1 AC 645

It was argued that the Southern Rhodesia Act 1965 had been passed contrary to constitutional convention (see Chapter 1).

Parliament had legislative supremacy and no court could hold an Act of Parliament invalid.

Lord Reid
'It is often said that it would be unconstitutional for ... Parliament to do certain things ... but that does not mean that it is beyond the power of Parliament to do such things. If Parliament chose to do any of them the courts could not hold the Act ... invalid.'

The judgment of the court follows the traditional notion of the doctrine of the supremacy of Parliament, as explained above. However, while Parliament could pass an Act invalidating any legislation passed in Southern Rhodesia, the effectiveness of that law is dependent upon it being enforced. The effectiveness of the Southern Rhodesia Act was limited by the fact that it was not enforced because of the territorial distance involved. Hence, while *de jure* power remained with the Westminster Parliament, *de facto* power was in the hands of the Rhodesian Government.

CA *Blackburn v AG* **[1971] 1 WLR 1037**

The appellant sought to challenge the accession of the UK to the Treaty of Rome.

The appellant was unsuccessful.

Lord Denning

' ... in legal theory, one Parliament cannot bind another and ... no Act is irreversible. But legal theory does not always march alongside political reality'.

Lord Denning recognises that legal theory must give way to what he terms 'practical politics'. He offers the example of Parliament trying to reverse grants of independence: 'freedom once given cannot be taken away'.

In *Manuel and Others v AG* [1983] Ch 77 (see above) Megarry VC comments that 'legal validity is one thing, enforceability is another'.

For discussion of the impact of membership of the European Union on parliamentary supremacy, see Chapter 7.

3.5.3 Constitutional statutes

 CA *Thoburn v Sunderland City Council*
[2002] 1 CMLR 50

 See Chapter 1 at **1.2**.

 Laws LJ
'We should recognise a hierarchy of Acts of Parliament: as it were "ordinary" statutes and "constitutional" statutes.'

'Ordinary statutes may be impliedly repealed. Constitutional statutes may not.'

 While the implied repeal doctrine still applies to most statutes, some senior judges regard it as inapplicable to statutes of major constitutional significance, which have to a certain extent become entrenched. For discussion of this in the context of the European Communities Act 1972, see Chapter 7.

In the context of the Human Rights Act 1998, implied repeal is effectively removed because if Parliament wants to legislate contrary to the European Convention on Human Rights it will only succeed if it uses express words or makes it extremely clear that is its intention. This is the effect of the duty of interpretation imposed on the courts by s 3 of the Act. Statements of compatibility under s 19 of the Act are useful in this context since they clarify the intention of Parliament in terms of its compliance with existing human rights obligations. For further discussion, see Chapter 9.

CHAPTER 4

PARLIAMENT

- Eligibility to vote
Hirst v UK (No2) **(2005)**
- Boundary Commission/Committees
R v Boundary Commission for England, ex parte Foot **(1983)**
- Conduct of election campaigns
Ashby v White **(1703)**
R v Tronah Mines Ltd **(1952)**
DPP v Luft **(1977)**
Walker v Unison **(1995)**
Grieve v Douglas-Home **(1965)**
- Broadcasting and election campaigns
R v BBC, ex parte Referendum Party **(1997)**
R (on the application of Pro-Life Alliance) v BBC **(2003)**
- Disputed elections
Gough v Local Sunday Newspapers (North) Ltd **(2003)**

Electoral law ◄——— PARLIAMENT ———► Privilege

- Freedom of speech and proceedings in Parliament
Rivlin v Bilainkin **(1953)**
Duncan Sandys' Case **(1938)**
Strauss and the London Electricity Board **(1956)**
R v Rule **(1937)**
A v UK **(2002)**
- The courts and privilege
Stockdale v Hansard **(1839)**
Pepper v Hart **(1983)**
- Composition and procedure in Parliament
Bradlaugh v Gosset **(1884)**

4.1 Electoral law

4.1.1 Eligibility to vote

 Hirst v UK (No2) [2005] BHRR 441

Under s 3 Representation of the People Act 1983, persons convicted of a criminal offence and detained in a penal institution in pursuance of a sentence are not eligible to vote.

The blanket exclusion of prisoners violates the right to free elections (see Art 3 of the First Protocol to the ECHR); there was no legitimate policy reason for excluding all convicted prisoners.

The Government has engaged in a consultation exercise since this decision to identify how best to proceed and a variety of reforms are under consideration.

4.1.2 Boundary Commission (now Committees)

 Harper v Secretary of State for the Home Department [1955] Ch 238

The method of calculating the electoral quota for England under the House of Commons (Redistribution of Seats) Act 1949 was challenged.

The Court of Appeal concluded that it would only intervene in such matters if the Act had been completely disregarded, which was not the case.

R v Boundary Commission for England, ex parte Foot
[1983] QB 600

The Boundary Commission made recommendations that the Labour Party believed had been based on misinterpretation of the rules for determining constituency boundaries.

The Commission has wide discretion in interpreting how much priority should be given to achieving arithmetical equality between constituencies given other factors. The courts will not intervene unless there is sufficient evidence to establish that the Commission has acted unreasonably.

The court's reluctance to oversee the Boundary Commission's recommendations must be seen in light of the fact that it is a politically sensitive matter, which is more appropriately dealt with by Parliament.

R v Secretary of State for the Home Department, ex parte McWhirter (1969) *The Times*, 20 October

4.1.3 Conduct of election campaigns

 Ashby v White (1703) 2 Ld Raym 938

Ashby was refused the right to vote by the returning officer, who he sued for damages.

The returning officer had acted wrongfully and damages were given.

Holt CJ
'To allow this action will make public officers more careful to observe the constitution of cities and boroughs, and not to be so partial as they commonly are in all elections.'

Section 63 of the Representation of the People Act 1983 (RPA 1983) places the responsibility of an official connected with the conduct of an election to act impartially on a statutory basis. Failure to do so attracts criminal penalties; such an official can no longer be sued for damages.

CA *R v Tronoh Mines Ltd* [1952] 1 All ER 697

Tronoh Mines placed an advertisement in *The Times*, urging voters not to vote socialist. They were charged under s 75 RPA 1983, which provides that no expenditure can be made other than by the candidate or their election agent.

It was held that the expenditure had been incurred with the intention of promoting the interests of a party generally, and not an individual candidate. Hence, any advantage incurred was accidental and the expenditure did not come within s 75.

One important factor, as highlighted in this case, is ensuring what was described in *R v Jones* [1999] 2 Cr App R 253 as a 'level financial playing field ... so as to prevent perversion of the voters' democratic choice between competing candidates within constituencies by significant disparities of local expenditure'. Considerable legislation has been introduced to try and ensure that elections are fair. This includes the Political Parties Elections and Referendums Act 2000 which introduced for the first time a limit on party campaign spending at a national level. It is an offence to exceed the limits, which are set by reference to the number of candidates fielded by a party and the type of election, whether national or regional. The limits do not apply to local government elections.

DPP v Luft [1977] AC 962

An anti-fascist group distributed pamphlets urging voters not to vote for National Front candidates. They were prosecuted under s 75 of the RPA 1983 for incurring expenditure with the aim of promoting election of a candidate without the authority of an election agent.

An offence had been committed – it was irrelevant that the group was seeking to prevent, rather than promote, the election of a candidate.

Walker v Unison [1995] SLT 1225

In Scotland, a Trade Union placed advertisements urging voters not to vote Conservative. No permission had been given by an election agent.

The advertisements were a general attack on a political party and not a direct attack on specific candidates and therefore they did not contravene the RPA 1983.

Grieve v Douglas-Home [1965] SLT 186

Douglas-Home's election was alleged to be void on the basis that he had participated in a national Party Political Broadcast for the Conservative Party and had not declared the expenditure.

No offence had been committed; the intention behind the broadcast was to provide general information about the party, not to promote the candidate.

4.1.4 Broadcasting and election campaigns

`DC` *R v BBC, ex parte Referendum Party* (1997) *The Times*, 29 April

The Referendum Party was allocated only one five-minute broadcast on each network and sought judicial review of this decision on the basis that as a new party the broadcasting

authorities should not have relied on past electoral support when allocating time.

Former electoral support was not a determining factor, but the broadcasting authorities could consider it as one criterion when allocating broadcasting time. The decision made was not irrational in the circumstances.

R v Broadcasting Complaints Commission, ex parte Owen [1985] QB 1153.

HL **R (on the application of Pro-Life Alliance) v BBC**
[2003] UKHL 23

The BBC refused to transmit the Alliance Party's election broadcast, on the basis that it was offensive and indecent.

The Court of Appeal held that it had to protect freedom of speech under the Human Rights Act 1998. The House of Lords disagreed, concluding that the BBC and other broadcasters had the right to refuse to show the broadcast on the basis that it would be offensive.

It is unlikely that a court will intervene with the broadcasting authority's decision, except in cases of bad faith or clear irrationality.

R (on the application of Pro-Life Alliance) v BBC [2003] UKHL
23 (see Chapter 8 at **8.1.1**).

4.1.5 Disputed elections

 Gough v Local Sunday Newspapers (North) Ltd
[2003] 2 All ER 456

The solicitor to Bedford Borough Council approved the
informal count of postal ballots that had not been discovered
until after the election had been declared.

Informal counts of ballot papers should not take place under
any circumstances.

In *Ruffle v Rogers* [1982] 3 WLR 143 the election papers had
been incorrectly counted and because this affected the result
the court held the election void. In *Knight v Nicholls* [2004]
1 WLR 1653 a large number of ballot papers had not been
delivered in time for the election, however it was held that the
returning officer had discharged his functions appropriately
and the election was valid.

4.2 Parliamentary privilege

4.2.1 Freedom from arrest

HC *Stourton v Stourton* [1963] P 302

A peer failed to send his wife her property under a court order. His arrest was sought for contempt of court.

The arrest was being sought to compel performance of a civil obligation against which a member of either House is protected.

The privilege to be free from arrest extends only to civil proceedings; members of both Houses have no privilege from arrest in the context of criminal proceedings.

4.2.2 Freedom of speech and 'proceedings in Parliament'

HC *Rivlin v Bilainkin* [1953] 1 QB 485

In breach of an injunction, the defendant repeated defamatory remarks in letters taken to the House of Commons. It was argued that the libel was committed within the precincts of the House of Commons and was therefore not actionable because it was privileged.

Freedom of speech is protected under Art XI of the Bill of Rights 1688 for 'debates and proceedings in Parliament'. The court held that the letters in question were not privileged because they were not connected in any way with proceedings in the House.

Duncan Sandys' Case (1938) – decision of Select Committee

Sandys sent a letter to a Minister that contained information that could only have been obtained via a breach of the Official Secrets Acts 1911–1920. A Select Committee was established to examine the situation.

Key findings of the Select Committee

The Committee Report concluded that privilege extends to all proceedings in Parliament, which includes everything said or done by an MP exercising their functions in either House in the transaction of parliamentary business. It did not generally extend to words or things done by an MP outside of Parliament, including a casual conversation in the House. However, situations could be privileged even though they did not take place within the House, such as communication between an MP and a Minister about business that would be tabled, or a draft question.

Strauss and the London Electricity Board
(1956) – decision of Select Committee

Strauss, an MP, forwarded a letter from a constituent to the relevant Minister in which there was criticism of the Board.

The Minister passed the letter to the Board, which threatened to sue Strauss for libel. The MP believed the matter was part of his parliamentary duties and therefore privileged.

Key findings of the Committee of Privileges
The letter was a proceeding in Parliament and therefore privileged.

The House of Commons disagreed with the Committee. However, the resolution is not binding on either the courts or the Commons itself.

The meaning of a 'proceeding in Parliament' remains in some contexts unclear and there have been numerous calls for the term to be defined in statute. In 1999 the Nicholls Committee produced a definition which did not extend absolute privilege to such letters – they would attract qualified privilege (see below).

In *Church of Scientology v Johnson Smith* [1972] 1 QB 522 the High Court held that parliamentary privilege excluded a course of action based on examination of proceedings in Parliament to support action arising out of something done outside the House.

 R v Rule [1937] 2 KB 375

A letter written by a constituent to an MP complained about the conduct of a police officer and a magistrate, forming the basis of an action for libel.

The court held that where a communication was made in the common interest, it would have qualified privilege (it is protected from liability unless malice is proved).

In *Beach v Freeson* [1972] 1 QB 14 a letter from an MP to the Lord Chancellor and the Law Society was protected under qualified privilege on the basis of public interest.

In *Rost v Edwards* [1950] 2 WLR 1280 the Register of Members' Interests was held not to be privileged.

CHR *A v UK* [2002] All ER (D) 264 (Dec)

The applicant contended that remarks made about her and her family in a debate were defamatory. These comments had been reported in the media. The comments were privileged under Art XI and hence immune from the law of defamation. She contended that this breached Art 6 (right to a fair trial), Art 8 (respect for private life) and Art 13 (right to an effective remedy) of the ECHR.

The European Court of Human Rights concluded that the rules of privilege were necessary to protect free speech in Parliament and there was no violation of the Convention.

It should be noted that the Court also pointed out that the British rules on privilege were in fact much narrower in scope than in many other countries.

4.2.3 The courts and privilege

QBD *Stockdale v Hansard* (1839) 9 Ad & E 1

Stockdale bought a series of actions against Hansard, for defamation. In the second case the defendant contended that the information had been published pursuant to a resolution of the House that publishing such reports was protected by privilege and that the House of Commons had the sole authority to determine the existence and extent of its privileges.

The court held that a resolution of the House could not prevent it from investigating the matter and that it could examine both the existence and extent of any privilege.

Lord Denman CJ

'It is said the House of Commons is the sole judge of its own privileges ... but I do not think it follows that they have a power to declare what their privileges are, so as to preclude enquiry.'

In *Rost v Edwards* [1950] 2 WLR 1280 Popplewell J commented that in grey areas concerning 'proceedings in Parliament' the courts should have jurisdiction to examine the matter. Conversely, if Parliament wished to extend privilege it should do so expressly within an Act of Parliament, thereby ousting the jurisdiction of the courts to examine the matter.

Case of the Sheriff of Middlesex (1840) 11 A & E 273.

HL *Pepper v Hart* [1983] 2 WLR 1032

There was a question as to whether parliamentary materials, such as *Hansard,* could be used by the courts to aid in the interpretation of statute, in this case s 63 Finance Act 1976, or whether such materials were privileged.

Hansard could be consulted to identify the intention of Parliament when passing a statute.

Lord Browne-Wilkinson

' … the use of clear ministerial statements by the court as a guide to the construction of ambiguous legislation would not contravene [Art 9 of the Bill of Rights]'.

In *Wilson v First County Trust Ltd (No 2)* [2003] UKHL 40 the House of Lords in *obiter* extended the judgment so that explanatory notes could also be considered. See also *Prebble v Television New Zealand Ltd* [1994] 3 All ER 407.

4.2.4 Composition and procedure of Parliament

QBD *Bradlaugh v Gosset* (1884) 12 QBD 271

Bradlaugh, a well-known atheist, was elected as an MP but the Speaker refused to let him take the oath of allegiance to the monarch. The House of Commons resolved to exclude him from the House. On trying to enter, he was ejected by Gosset, the Sargeant-at-Arms. Bradlaugh sought an injunction against the Sargeant and a declaration that the resolution was void.

Internal management of the House is a matter of privilege that the courts have no jurisdiction to consider.

Lord Coleridge CJ
'What is said or done within the walls of Parliament cannot be enquired into in a court of law … The jurisdiction of the Houses over their own members, their right to impose discipline … is absolute and exclusive.'

Interference by the courts into the internal affairs of Parliament would be contempt of Parliament.

In *Re Parliamentary Election for Bristol South East* [1964] 2 QB 257 the House refused to let Tony Benn MP take his seat because he had succeeded to a peerage. He was only able to so after renouncing his title under the Peerage Act 1963.

CHAPTER 5

CENTRAL GOVERNMENT

Ministerial responsibility

Carltona Ltd v Works Commissioners **(1943)** and *Crichel Down Affair* **(1953)** – a Minister is responsible to Parliament for the conduct of their department

Ministerial Code: A Code of Conduct and Guidance on Procedure for Ministers 2001 – modern explanation of ministerial accountability

The Royal Prerogative

Case of Proclamations **(1611)** and *Case of Ship Money* **(1637)**
Cases curtailing the law-making powers of the Crown
AG v de Keyser's Royal Hotel Ltd **(1920)**
Laker Airways v Department of Trade **(1977)**
R v Secretary of State for the Home Department, ex parte Fire Brigades' Union and Others **(1995)**
Cases examining the relationship between statute and the prerogative
R v Secretary of State for the Home Department, ex parte Northumbria Police Authority **(1989)**
The use of prerogatives in modern contexts

R v Criminal Injuries Compensation Board, ex parte Lain **(1967)**
CCSU v Minister of State for the Civil Service **(1985)**
Some prerogative powers are reviewable by the courts, depending on their subject-matter; matters of high policy are non-reviewable.

Example – pardons
R v Bentley **(1998)**
Example – treaty-making powers
R v Secretary of State for Foreign and Commonwealth Affairs, ex parte Rees-Mogg **(1994)**
Example – issuing passports
R v Secretary of State for Foreign and Commonwealth Affairs, ex parte Everett **(1989)**
Example – declaring war, deployment of troops
CND v Prime Minister **(2002)**

5.1 Conventions of ministerial responsibility

Carltona Ltd v Works Commissioners [1943] 2 All ER 560

Under wartime regulations, the Commissioners requisitioned Carltona's property. The order was signed by a civil servant.

A Minister can lawfully delegate power to a subordinate but remains, under convention, accountable to Parliament for the conduct of his department.

Lord Greene MR

'In the administration of government ... the functions which are given to ministers ... are functions so multifarious that no minister could ever personally attend to them ... The duties imposed ... and the powers given to ministers are normally exercised ... by responsible officials ... Constitutionally the decision of ... an officer is the decision of the minister. The minister is responsible. It is he who must answer before Parliament'.

Crichel Down Affair (1953) Cmnd 9220 1954 HMSO

Crichel Down had been compulsorily purchased in 1937. After the Second World War the land was not needed and was transferred to the Ministry of Agriculture and administered by a Commission. The owner wanted to reclaim the land and raised the matter with his MP. The MP referred the matter to the Minister's Parliamentary Secretary, who requested a report from the Commission. The report was inaccurate and was not checked by the Ministry. The owner was informed in 1953 that the land would be turned into a farm and he stated he would rent it. Meanwhile, the Ministry decided to do something else with the land. The owner requested a public inquiry.

Key findings

The inquiry found that the report was inaccurate and the matter had been dealt with in an inefficient manner.

In 1954 the Minister, Thomas Dugdale, accepted responsibility and resigned. In the debate the Home Secretary, Sir David Maxwell Fyfe, stated that a Minister was under a duty to defend a civil servant carrying out his explicit order or policy. If a civil servant acts in a reprehensible manner without the Minister's knowledge then the Minister is not obligated to defend them but remains 'constitutionally responsible to Parliament for the fact that something has gone wrong'.

The modern basis for ministerial responsibility can now be found in the **Ministerial Code: A Code of Conduct and Guidance on Procedure for**

Ministers (Cabinet Office 2001), which states in paragraph 1:

'(1) Ministers have a duty to Parliament to account and to be held to account, for the policies, decisions and actions of their Departments and Next Step Agencies;

(2) It is of paramount importance that Ministers give accurate and truthful information to Parliament, correcting any inadvertent error at the earliest opportunity. Ministers who knowingly mislead will be expected to offer their resignation to the Prime Minister;

(3) Ministers should be as open as possible with Parliament, refusing to provide information only when disclosure would not be in the public interest ... ;

(4) Similarly, Ministers should require civil servants who give evidence before Parliamentary Committees on their behalf and under their directions to be as helpful as possible in providing accurate, truthful and full information'.

There is therefore no duty on a Minister to resign. Whether they do so or not appears to depend on a range of political factors such as whether they have party support; the response of the Prime Minister; and the Minister's own character. Such factors can, of course, be heavily influenced by the media.

5.2 Royal Prerogative

5.2.1 Curtailment of the law-making powers of the Crown

Case of Proclamations (1611) 12 Co Rep 74; 77 ER 1352

See Chapter 3 at **3.1**.

The monarch does not have the power to create law by proclamation.

Chief Justice Coke

' ... the King by his proclamation or other ways cannot change any part of the common law, or statute law, or the customs of the realm.

... the King cannot create any offence by his prohibition or proclamation, which was not an offence before ...

... the King hath no prerogative but that which the law of the land allows him.'

In *Prohibitions del Roy (Case of Prohibitions)* (1607) 12 Co Rep 63 the King claimed the right to dispense justice in his own right. In the Resolution of the Judges, Chief Justice Coke stated that 'the King in his own person cannot adjudge any case ... this ought to be determined ... in some court of justice'.

Case of Ship Money (R v Hampden) (1637) 3 St Tr 825

See Chapter 3 at **3.1**.

The courts upheld the power of the Crown.

The decision was reversed by the Shipmoney Act 1640. Art IV of the Bill of Rights 1688 made it illegal for the Crown to raise revenue without Parliament's approval.

The Stuart monarchs' claims to rule by prerogative powers were resolved by the Bill of Rights 1688, under which Parliament became the supreme law-making authority. From this time the prerogative powers of the Crown could continue, or be controlled by Parliament; no new ones could be claimed by the Crown.

In *BBC v Johns* [1964] 1 All ER 923 [1965] Ch 32 Lord Diplock recognised this when he stated that it was '350 years and a civil war too late ... to broaden the prerogative. The limits within which the executive government may impose obligations or restraints on citizens of the United Kingdom without any statutory authority are now well settled and incapable of extension'.

(For discussion of the difficulties inherent in using such ancient prerogatives in the modern context, see below at **5.2.3**.)

5.2.2 Statute and the prerogative

HL *AG v de Keyser's Royal Hotel Ltd* [1920] AC 508

The War Office took over the hotel, claiming to act under statute that gave the owners a right to claim compensation. At a later date the War Office claimed to have acted under the Royal Prerogative, providing no automatic right to compensation.

The Crown had acted expressly under the statute. But in any event, where statute and prerogative exist on the same subject-matter, the prerogative cannot be used (it is ousted or in abeyance) unless preserved by express provision.

Lord Atkinson

' ... after the statute has been passed, and while it is in force, the thing it empowers the Crown to do can thenceforth only be done by and under the statute, and subject to all the limitations, restrictions and conditions by it imposed, however unrestricted the Royal Prerogative may theretofore have been ... '.

Where prerogative and statute exist on the same subject-matter, the statute will oust the prerogative. The only exception to this is where a statute expressly permits the prerogative to continue. If the statute is later repealed the prerogative power will come back into use, unless the repealing statute expressly states that it is not to be revived: see *Burmah Oil v Lord Advocate* [1965] AC 75 and *R v Secretary of State for Foreign and Commonwealth Affairs, ex parte CCSU* [1984] IRLR 309.

CA *Laker Airways v Department of Trade* [1977] QB 643

The Civil Aviation Act 1971 provided for the licensing of airlines by the Civil Aviation Authority (CAA) under guidance from the Secretary of State. Laker applied for a licence and for a designation under the Bermuda Agreement 1946 so that he could fly to the USA. A change of government led to a change in policy. The Government claimed that it had power under the prerogative to deny Laker the ability to fly to the USA.

The Secretary of State had acted *ultra vires* in that guidance he had given the CAA was beyond that provided for under the statute. The use of the prerogative to stop flights to the USA was not supported.

Prerogative powers cannot be used in such a way as to defeat the purpose of statute.

CA *R v Secretary of State for the Home Department, ex parte Fire Brigades' Union and Others* [1995] 2 WLR 1

The Home Secretary decided not to implement a scheme for compensation under the Criminal Justice Act 1988 and wanted to set one up under prerogative powers that provided for lower levels of compensation.

While in force, the prerogative cannot be used to frustrate the purposes of statute.

Sir Thomas Bingham MR
' ... what [the Home Secretary] could not do, so long as the
1988 provisions stood unrepealed ... was to exercise
prerogative powers to introduce a scheme radically different
from what Parliament had approved.'

5.2.3 'New' prerogatives

 *R v Secretary of State for the Home Department, ex parte
Northumbria Police Authority* [1989] QB 26

The Police Act 1964 set out the powers of the Home
Secretary, police authorities and Chief Constables to, *inter
alia*, supply equipment to police forces. The Home Secretary
sent out a circular that riot control equipment would be
provided regardless of police authority approval. The legality
of the circular was challenged.

The Police Act 1964 did not affect the prerogative power to keep
the peace. This prerogative was a sister prerogative to the power
to declare war. The Home Secretary had not acted illegally.

Purchas LJ
' ... the prerogative powers to take all reasonable steps to
preserve the Queen's peace remain unaffected by the Act.'

Prerogative powers are residual, hence to use such power
successfully it should have existed before the Bill of Rights

1688 (see *BBC v Johns* at **5.2.1**). In this case, however, there was no evidence to justify the claim that a prerogative to keep the peace existed.

This case shows the difficulties inherent in using old prerogatives in a modern context, since to do so could in reality create a new prerogative power.

5.2.4 Review of the exercise of prerogative powers

HC *R v Criminal Injuries Compensation Board,*
ex parte Lain **[1967] 2 QB 864**

The Board was set up under the prerogative to administer benefits for the victims of criminal injury. Lain challenged a decision of the Board.

The High Court could review the decisions of the Board; it was irrelevant that it was set up under the prerogative rather than statute.

Traditionally, the courts had examined the existence and extent of a prerogative power, but had not been prepared to consider the manner in which such powers were exercised. In this case there is the first indication of a change in this attitude, which can also be witnessed in comments made by Lord Denning in the *Laker* case (see **5.2.2**).

HL | *CCSU v Minister of State for the Civil Service*
[1985] AC 374 (GCHQ Case)

Prerogative empowered the Minister to issue instructions in respect of the conditions of service for civil servants. Following industrial action at the Government Communication Headquarters (GCHQ) the Minister issued instructions that barred membership of a Trade Union. Contrary to usual practice, the Minister did not consult with the Trade Union before issuing the instruction.

An exercise of prerogative power is susceptible to judicial review. In the case at hand, while the Union had a legitimate expectation to be consulted, on the facts this was outweighed by the interests of national security.

Lord Roskill

'If the executive … acts under a prerogative power … so as to affect the rights of the citizen, I am unable to see … that there is any logical reason why the fact that the source of the power is the prerogative and not statute should today deprive the citizen of that right of challenge to the manner of its exercise which he would possess were the source of the power statutory.'

This landmark decision extended judicial review to acts of the prerogative. However, the application of judicial review is limited or qualified.

Whether a particular prerogative power is amenable to review depends upon its nature and subject-matter. Lord Roskill identified a number of significant prerogative powers that by their very nature are not capable of being reviewed in terms of their use by the courts. These included:

- making treaties
- defence of the realm
- granting mercy
- granting honours
- dissolution of Parliament and
- ministerial appointment.

However, Lord Roskill also stated that 'other' prerogatives could also be non-reviewable. The following are examples of cases examining whether particular prerogative powers are amenable to judicial review.

Example – Pardons

The prerogative of mercy has traditionally been considered non-reviewable: *De Freitas v Benny* [1976] AC 239. Lord Roskill in *GCHQ* also considered this to be the case.

 R v Bentley [1998] TLR 31 July

In 1952, 19-year-old Bentley was convicted of the murder of a policeman (although another person had fired the fatal shot). He had the mental age of an 11-year-old. At the time, the mandatory sentence was the death penalty and Bentley was hanged. In 1992 the Home Secretary refused to grant a posthumous pardon. In an application for judicial review the court considered whether the prerogative of mercy was capable of review (*R v Secretary of State for the Home Department, ex parte Bentley* [1994] QB 349), concluding that 'some aspects' of the exercise of the mercy prerogative were amenable to review. The court did not make any formal order but invited the Home Secretary to reconsider the matter. In 1998 the

Criminal Cases Review Commission referred the case to the
Court of Appeal.

The court ruled the conviction unsafe on a number of
grounds. The conviction for murder was consequently
quashed.

Example – Treaty-making powers

The Executive holds the prerogative power to make treaties.

 CA ***R v Secretary of State for Foreign and Commonwealth
Affairs, ex parte Rees-Mogg* [1994] 2 WLR 115**

Rees-Mogg challenged the authority of the Government to
ratify the Treaty on European Union (Maastricht Treaty).

The application for judicial review was rejected; treaty making
was a non-reviewable prerogative power.

Blackburn v Attorney-General [1971] 1 WLR 1037; [1971] 2
All ER 1380.

Example – Issuing passports

Passports are issued under the prerogative.

R v Secretary of State for Foreign and Commonwealth Affairs, ex parte Everett [1989] QB 811

Everett was residing in Spain. His application to renew his passport was refused, but he was given no reasons. He challenged the decision by judicial review.

The court held that the granting and withholding of passports was subject to judicial review.

Taylor LJ
Issuing passports is a prerogative that is reviewable because it is a 'matter of administrative decision, affecting the rights of individuals and their freedom of travel'.

A distinction can be drawn between prerogatives involving matters of 'high' policy and those that are 'low' policy. The former were not subject to review, such as defence of the realm/national security. Matters of low policy, such as issuing passports, are subject to review particularly when they involve the rights of individuals at an administrative level.

Example – Declaring war and the deployment of troops

Campaign for Nuclear Disarmament v Prime Minister [2002] EWHR 2777

CND challenged the legality of the decision of the Government to send troops to Iraq.

Such matters are not reviewable by the courts.

Richards J
' … it is unthinkable that the national courts would entertain a challenge to a government decision to declare war or to authorise the use of armed forces against a third country. That is a classic example of a non-justiciable decision'.

CHAPTER 6

LAW OF THE EUROPEAN COMMUNITY

- Article 234/EC preliminary references

  Bulmer v Bollinger (1974)

- Supremacy of EC Law

  Van Gend en Loos v Nederlandse Tariefcommissie (1963)
  Costa v ENEL (1964)
  Internationale Handelsgesellschaft (1970)

- Direct effect

  Van Gend en Loos (1963)
  Van Duyn v Home Office (1975)
  Marshall v Southampton and SW Hampshire AHA (1986)
  Foster v British Gas (1991)

- Indirect effect

  Von Colson v Land Nordrhein-Westfalen (1984)

- State liability

  Francovich and Bonifaci v Italy (1991)
  Brasserie du Pêcheur joined with ex parte Factortame (No4) (1996)
  R v HM Treasury, ex parte BT (1996)
  R v Minister of Agriculture Fisheries and Food, ex parte Hedley Lomas (1996)
  Dillenkofer v Germany (1996)

6.1 Preliminary reference procedure (Art 234/EC)

 HC *Bulmer v Bollinger* [1974] Ch 401

An appeal was brought against the refusal of the High Court to make a preliminary reference under Art 234/EC (then Art 177).

When deciding whether to refer, the court should consider whether a decision on the matter is necessary to enable it to give judgment. When exercising this discretion the courts should take into account factors such as the length of time; the difficulty and significance of the point; the expense; and the wishes of the parties.

Lord Denning took a restrictive approach to making references and these 'guidelines' have been widely criticised. In *Customs and Excise Commissioners v ApS Samex* [1983] 3 All ER 1042 it was recognised that the ECJ was in a better position than the English courts to assess and determine points of EC law.

These guidelines were effectively reformulated in *R v International Stock Exchange, ex parte Else* [1993] QB 534. In this case Lord Bingham offered the following guidelines: if the matter is critical the court should ordinarily refer but there is no obligation to refer if the court can 'with complete confidence resolve the issue itself'. In deciding whether it can do this the court must take into consideration the differences between national and Community law; the need for uniform interpretation of EC law; and the advantageous position the ECJ is in interpreting EC law.

In *CILFIT & I v Ministro della Sanita* (Case 283/81) [1982] ECR 3415 the ECJ stated that a reference is not necessary if either the question of Community law is irrelevant or the point of Community law has already been interpreted by the Court of Justice. A reference is not necessary (*acte clair*) where:

' ... the correct application of Community law may be so obvious as to leave no scope for any reasonable doubt as to the manner in which the question raised is to be resolved. Before it comes to the conclusion that such is the case, the national court ... must be convinced that the matter was equally obvious to the courts of the other member states and to the Court of Justice'.

6.2 The supremacy of EC law

ECJ *Van Gend en Loos v Nederlandse Tariefcommissie*
(Case 26/62) [1963] ECR 1

 VGeL imported products from Germany into the Netherlands and was charged an increased customs duty contrary to Art 12 of the EEC Treaty (now Art 25/EC).

 The EEC (now EU) was a *sui generis* (unique) legal order and Member States had limited their sovereign rights when joining, hence EC law takes precedence over national law.

 ECJ preliminary reference
' ... the Community constitutes a new legal order ... for the benefit of which the states have limited their sovereign rights'.

The court used teleological (or purposive) interpretation to come to the conclusion that while the Treaty did not expressly state that EC law had supremacy, it was required in order for the Treaty to meet its objectives and purpose.

ECJ *Costa v ENEL* (Case 6/64) [1964] ECR 1125

Costa contended that Italian law breached the Treaty.

The Member States had limited their sovereign rights, were bound by Community law and Community law took precedence over conflicting national law.

ECJ preliminary reference
' … the law stemming from the Treaty … could not, because of its special and original nature, be overridden by domestic legal provisions … without being deprived of its character as Community law and without the legal basis of the Community itself being called into question'.

In *Amministrazione delle Finanze dello Stato v Simmenthal SpA* (Case 106/77) [1978] ECR 629 the Court of Justice stated that national courts are bound to apply Community law in its entirety and set aside any conflicting provision of national law regardless of whether it is prior or subsequent to Community law.

Internationale Handelsgesellschaft mbH v EVST
(Case 11/70) [1970] ECR 1125

It was contended that EC law, in the form of regulations that required forfeiture of a deposit if the terms of an import/export licence were breached, violated the German constitution.

EC law takes precedence over all forms of conflicting national law, including codified constitutional principles.

ECJ preliminary reference
'Recourse to the legal rules or concepts of national law in order to judge the validity of measures adopted by the institutions of the Community would have an adverse effect on the uniformity and efficacy of Community law. The validity of such measures can only be judged in the light of Community law. In fact, the law stemming from the Treaty, an independent source of law, cannot because of its very nature be overridden by rules of national law, however framed, without being deprived of its character as Community law and without the legal basis of the Community itself being called into question.'

See *R v Secretary of State for Transport, ex parte Factortame Ltd and Others* [1990] 2 AC 85 and *(No 2)* [1991] 1 AC 603 (see Chapter 7 at **7.2.2**).

6.3 Direct effect

ECJ *Van Gend en Loos v Nederlandse Tariefcommissie*
(Case 26/62) [1963] ECR 1

 See **6.2.**

 The Treaty creates rights for individuals that can
be enforced in their national legal system (direct
effect). To have direct effect, the EC measure must
be clear and precise, unconditional, and non-
dependent.

 ECJ preliminary reference
'Community law ... not only imposes obligations
on individuals but is also intended to confer on
them rights which become part of their legal
heritage.'

 There are two types of direct effect: vertical and
horizontal. Vertical direct effect means that the
measure is capable of being enforced against the
State; horizontal direct effect means that the
measure can be enforced against another natural or
legal person. This case is an example of a Treaty
provision having vertical direct effect.

 See *Defrenne v SABENA* (Case 43/75) [1978]
ECR 1365 for an example of a Treaty provision
(Art 141, ex Art 119) having horizontal direct
effect.

ECJ *Van Duyn v Home Office* (Case 41/74) [1975] 1 CMLR 1

Van Duyn challenged the decision to refuse her entry into the UK by referring to rights contained within Directive 64/221. In particular, that the Directive required any decision to refuse her entry to be based exclusively on her personal conduct.

A Directive may be capable of creating directly effective rights.

Directives are defined under Art 249/EC as being binding but they leave the choice of form and method to the Member State's discretion as to how the objective is achieved. On face value, therefore, Directives are dependent and would appear not to have direct effect. In order to ensure the maximum effect of EC law, the Court in this case decided to extend direct effect to Directives. However, since Directives are by their nature dependent, they are not capable of direct effect until the deadline for implementation has expired: *Pubblico Ministerio v Ratti* (Case 148/78) [1979] ECR 1629.

ECJ *Marshall v Southampton and South West Hampshire Area Health Authority (No 1)* (Case 152/84) [1986] QB 401

Marshall sought to enforce the terms of Directive 76/207 (the Equal Treatment Directive) against her employer.

Directives are capable of only vertical, and not horizontal, direct effect.

ECJ preliminary reference

' … a directive may not … impose obligations on an individual and … a provision of a directive may not be relied upon as against such a person'.

Faccini Dori v Recreb Srl (Case C-91/92) [1994] ECR I-3325.

ECJ *Foster v British Gas* (Case 188/89) [1991] 2 AC 306

Foster sought to rely on Directive 76/207 against her employer.

The 'State' was defined to include bodies that provide a public service, under the control of the State, and which have special powers beyond those that result from the normal rules applicable in relations between individuals.

The English courts stated in *National Union of Teachers v Governing Body of St Mary's Church of England (Aided) Junior School* [1997] IRLR 242 that the *Foster* test should not be authoritative and should be a broad one. The ECJ reconsidered the definition of the State in *Kampelmann v*

Landschaftsverband Westfalenlippe and Others [1997] ECR I-6907, the test being whether the body in question:

- is controlled or regulated by the State or
- has special powers or
- under public authority, provides a public service.

6.4 Indirect effect

Von Colson and Kamann v Land Nordrhein-Westfalen (Case 14/83) [1984] ECR 1891

The applicants sought compensation for being refused employment. Under German law this was limited to travelling expenses and it was contended that this was not compatible with the provisions of Directive 76/207.

The national courts are under an obligation stemming from Art 10 EC to ensure that all appropriate measures are taken to ensure the attainment of Community law obligations. The duty of the courts is to therefore interpret national law in such a way as to ensure that it is compatible with Community law.

If a provision of EC law does not have direct effect or in the case of directives cannot be enforced because of the lack of horizontal direct effect it may be applied indirectly through this process of interpretation.

In *Marleasing SA v La Commercial Internacional de Alimentacion SA* (Case 106/89) [1992] 1 CMLR 305 the ECJ ruled that national courts must, as far as possible, interpret national law so that it is compatible with any relevant directive, regardless of whether the national provisions were adopted prior to or after the directive.

6.5 State liability

 Francovich and Bonifaci v Italy (Cases C-6, C-9/90) [1991] ECR I-5357

The applicants could not rely on the terms of a directive that had not been implemented by Italy, since it did not have direct effect because it lacked clarity and precision. Instead, they sought to claim damages for loss they had incurred because of the failure by the Italian Government to implement the directive.

The court concluded that damages could be awarded against the Italian Government for failing to implement the directive under the following criteria:

* the directive intended to confer rights on individuals
* the content of those rights was identifiable and
* there was a causal link between the breach of the directive and the damage sustained.

ECJ preliminary reference
' ... the principle whereby a State must be liable for loss and damage caused to individuals as a result of breaches of Community law for which the State can be held responsible is inherent in the system of the Treaty'.

This landmark decision was the first case to determine that the State could be liable to individuals for breaches of Community law. However, the criteria to establish liability were altered by the following case.

 Brasserie du Pêcheur SA v Federal Republic of Germany (Cases C-46/93, C-48/93) [1996] ECR I-1029; joined with *R v Secretary of State for Transport, ex parte Factortame Ltd* (No 4) (Joined cases C-46/93 and C-48/93) [1996] 2 WLR 506

Brasserie and Factortame sought to establish the liability of the German and British Governments respectively for breaches of the EC Treaty.

State liability is established under the following criteria:

- whether the law infringed creates rights for individuals
- whether the breach is 'sufficiently serious' and
- whether there is a causal link between the breach and the damage sustained by the individual.

A breach is sufficiently serious when the State is considered to have manifestly and gravely disregarded the limits of its discretion. In determining whether this is the case the national court can consider a number of factors such as the clarity and precision of the measure breached; the measure of discretion left to the national authorities; whether the action was intentional or involuntary; whether a Community institution contributed to the breach; and whether national measures in conflict with EC law were adopted or retained.

This case introduces the notion of a threshold level of seriousness before liability can be established. The State therefore has the opportunity to avoid liability for a breach of Community law on the basis that it lacks the degree of seriousness required. The burden of proof to establish the causal link is on the individual.

In *R v Secretary of State for Transport, ex parte Factortame Ltd (No 5)* [2000] 1 AC 524 Lord Slynn concluded that the 'deliberate adoption of legislation which was clearly discriminatory on the grounds of nationality and which inevitably violated … the Treaty' was a sufficiently serious breach.

The definition of the 'State' for the purposes of State liability is a broad one (see **6.3**) and extends to the courts: *Köbler v Republic of Austria* (Case C-224/01) [2004] 2 WLR 976.

 ECJ *R v HM Treasury, ex parte BT plc* **(Case C-392/93) [1996] ECR I-1631**

The UK incorrectly implemented a directive and BT claimed that this had caused the company financial loss.

The UK was not liable because the breach was not sufficiently serious. The Directive lacked clarity and precision and the UK's interpretation had been a reasonable one. The UK had acted in 'good faith'.

Denkavit International BV v Bundesamt für Finanzen (Cases C-283, 291 and 292/94) [1996] ECR I-5063, *Brinkman Tabakfabriken GmbH v Skatteministeriet* (Case C-319/96) [1998] ECR I-5255 and *Rechberger and Greindle v Austria* (Case C-140/97) [1999] ECR I-3499.

 R v Ministry of Agriculture, Fisheries and Food, ex parte Hedley Lomas (Ireland) Ltd [1996] ECR I-2553

Hedley Lomas claimed that it had suffered loss as a result of the UK's ban on the transportation of live sheep in breach of the EC Treaty. The UK claimed that the breach was justified to protect animal health because Spain was not complying with a directive on the stunning of animals prior to slaughter.

In some instances, such as in this case, the mere infringement of Community law may constitute an automatically sufficiently serious breach.

The Court has taken an inconsistent approach in some cases and has not applied the test set out in *Brasserie*. In this case the Court concluded that the State was *per se* liable because it was a situation in which it had no legislative choices to make and had considerably reduced, or no, discretion.

Norbrook Laboratories Ltd v Minister of Agriculture, Fisheries and Food (Case C-127/95) [1998] ECR I-1531.

ECJ *Dillenkofer v Federal Republic of Germany* [1996] ECR I–4845

Germany failed to implement a directive by its deadline. Dillenkofer claimed that she had suffered financial loss as a result of this.

The failure to implement a directive by its deadline was *per se* sufficiently serious.

All that need be established in such a case is that there is a causal link between the failure to implement and the damage sustained. The onus of proving this rests on the individual.

CHAPTER 7

MEMBERSHIP OF THE EU AND PARLIAMENTARY SUPREMACY

EEC TREATY (now EC Treaty)

↓

Dualist nature of UK legal system
Blackburn v AG **(1971)**
<u>**EUROPEAN COMMUNITIES ACT 1972**</u>

↓

Section 2(4) Acts passed *or to be passed* must be
compatible with EC law

ACTS NOT IN FULL
CONFORMITY WITH
EC LAW

↓

Macarthys v Smith **(1979)**
Garland v BREL **(1982)**
Duke v GEC Reliance Systems **(1988)**
Webb v EMO Air Cargo Ltd **(1992)**

ACTS DIRECTLY
BREACHING EC LAW

↓

Factortame (No 1) **(1990)**
Factortame (No 2) **(1991)**

↓

REMOVAL OF IMPLIED REPEAL

↓

RETENTION OF EXPRESS REPEAL
Macarthys v Smith **(1979)**
Garland v BREL **(1982)**

7.1 The European Communities Act 1972

 CA *Blackburn v Attorney-General* [1971] 1 WLR 1037

Blackburn sought a declaration that the Government acted unlawfully in signing the EEC Treaty since it would surrender parliamentary supremacy and bind a future Parliament, contrary to constitutional principles (see Chapter 3).

A Treaty may be signed but it will have no effect within the UK until incorporated by an Act of Parliament.

Lord Denning

'Even if a Treaty is signed, it is elementary that these courts take no notice of treaties as such. We take no notice of treaties until they are embodied in laws enacted by Parliament, and then only to the extent that Parliament tells us.'

The UK is a dualist legal system, within which only national law may be directly applied. Treaties may be signed by the Government as an act of the Royal Prerogative (which is not subject to judicial review, see Chapter 5) but to be applied by the courts must be incorporated or implemented into UK law by an Act of Parliament. For example, the European Convention of Human Rights was incorporated by the Human Rights Act 1998. Thus, the EEC Treaty required the passing of statute to have full effect, in this case the European Communities Act 1972.

In *R v Secretary of State for the Home Department, ex parte McWhirter* (1969) *The Times*, 20 October Lord Denning stated 'even though the Treaty of Rome has been signed, it has no effect as far as the courts are concerned until implemented by Act of Parliament. Until that day, we take no notice of it'. See also *R v Secretary of State for Foreign and Commonwealth Affairs, ex parte Rees-Mogg* [1994] 2 WLR 115(see Chapter 5 at **5.2.4**).

7.2 Section 2(4) European Communities Act 1972 and the courts

7.2.1 Acts not in full conformity with EC Law – the rule of construction

 Macarthys v Smith [1979] 3 All ER 32

Macarthys argued that being paid less than a man who had previously held her job was a violation of the EC Treaty, which provides for equal pay for men and women for equal work (ex Art 119, now Art 141). The Equal Pay Act 1970, as amended by the Sex Discrimination Act 1975, was unclear on this point. Section 2(4) of the European Communities Act 1972, however, required all legislation passed or to be passed to be compatible with directly enforceable Community law.

Section 2(1) and (4) of the European Communities Act 1972 place an obligation on the courts to construe national legislation so that it is compatible with Community law.

Lord Denning

'In construing our statute, we are entitled to look to the
Treaty as an aid in its construction: and even more, not only
as an aid, but as an overriding force. If on close investigation it
should appear that our legislation is deficient – or is
inconsistent with Community law ... it is our bounden duty
to give priority to Community law.'

The obligation to interpret national law in light of
Community law is referred to as a 'rule of construction'.

HL *Garland v BREL* [1982] ECR 359

British Rail permitted the children of only male
employees reaching retirement to have
concessionary travel. This was challenged as
contrary to the EC Treaty. The Equal Pay Act
1970 was silent on this point.

The approach of Lord Denning in the *Macarthys*
case was adopted by the House of Lords in
interpreting the Act.

Lord Diplock
' ... it is a principle of construction of United
Kingdom statutes ... that the words of a statute
passed after the Treaty ... and dealing with the
same subject matter ... are to be construed if they
are reasonably capable of bearing such a meaning,
as intended to carry out the obligation, and not to
be inconsistent with it'.

One difficulty is the extent to which a court may interpret domestic legislation so that it is compatible with Community law – Lord Diplock refers to the obligation extending only to the point that the interpretation is 'reasonable'.

HL | *Duke v GEC Reliance Systems Ltd* [1988] 1 AC 618

Duke challenged differing retirement ages permitted under the Sex Discrimination Act 1975 as being in breach of the Equal Treatment Directive. The Directive could not be imposed against the private company (see Chapter 6). It was contended that, under s 2(4) of the European Communities Act 1972, the Act should be construed so that it was compatible with the Directive.

Section 2(4) of the 1972 Act did not permit a court to construe an Act in a way that would permit the terms of a Directive to be enforced against an individual.

The *Macarthys* and *Garland* cases show the English courts' effective acceptance of what is known in EC law as indirect effect (discussed in Chapter 6). The decision in *Duke* is not consistent with the EC obligation to interpret national law in the light of Directives, as established in *Marleasing SA v La Commercial Internacional de Alimentacion SA* (Case 106/89) [1992] 1 CMLR 305 (see Chapter 6 at **6.4**). However, since *Duke*, the House of Lords has revealed increasing willingness to undertake the 'interpretative obligation', as witnessed in the following case.

Webb v EMO Air Cargo (UK) Ltd [1992] 4 All ER 929

The claimant contended that her dismissal after informing her employer of her pregnancy was in breach of the Equal Treatment Directive.

A court should construe a statute so that it complies with the terms of a Directive, irrespective of whether the statute was passed before or after it.

Similarly, in *Litster v Forth Dry Dock Ltd* [1990] 1 AC 546 the House of Lords interpreted a UK regulation in a manner clearly contrary to its clear meaning, in order to ensure its compatibility with an EC Directive.

The extent of the courts' willingness to construe legislation in such a way is perhaps most clearly witnessed in *Pickstone v Freemans plc* [1989] AC 66, where the House of Lords departed from a literal interpretation of the UK law and implied words to plug gaps in the legislation so that it was compatible with Community law.

7.2.2 Direct conflict between EC law and statute

HL | *R v Secretary of State for Transport, ex parte Factortame* (No 1) [1990] 2 AC 85 and (No 2) [1991] 1 AC 603

Spanish fishing vessels had been registered in the UK so that they could take advantage of British fishing quotas. In 1988 the UK passed the Merchant Shipping Act 1988, which introduced a licensing system. This required applicants, *inter alia*, to have a genuine and substantial connection with the UK. The conditions made it effectively impossible for Factortame to obtain the licence.

The European Commission brought an enforcement action in the ECJ for breach of the EC Treaty (the right to establish a company and the right to freedom from discrimination on the basis of nationality) and the ECJ ordered the UK to suspend the offending sections of the Merchant Shipping Act. Meanwhile, Factortame bought proceedings under judicial review in the English courts, requesting interim relief in the form of an injunction against the Secretary of State preventing its deregistration.

The House of Lords, following the Court of Appeal, concluded that there was no power in English law to grant interim relief, since to do so would imply that the Act was invalid, contrary to the principles of parliamentary supremacy. However, the House of Lords requested a preliminary reference as to whether it was obliged under Community law to protect Community rights and grant interim relief.

The ECJ referred to the principle that Community law must take precedence over conflicting national law and by fully and uniformly applied. The Court concluded that any principle of national law preventing interim relief should be set aside.

 In *Factortame (No 2)* the House of Lords accepted the ECJ's ruling in that Community law must take precedence over directly conflicting national law and granted interim relief, suspending operation of Part II of the Merchant Shipping Act.

 Lord Bridge
'If the supremacy ... of Community law over the national law of member states was not always inherent in the EEC Treaty it was certainly well established in the jurisprudence of the Court of Justice long before the United Kingdom joined the Community. Thus, whatever limitation of its sovereignty Parliament accepted when it enacted the European Communities Act 1972 was entirely voluntary. Under the terms of the 1972 Act it has always been clear that it was the duty of a United Kingdom court ... to override any rule of national law found to be in conflict with any directly enforceable rule of Community law.'

 This case was the first to reach the courts where there was a direct conflict between national and Community law and which could not be rectified using the interpretative method adopted in *Macarthys* and *Garland*. The response of the ECJ was entirely consistent with its previous jurisprudence on the supremacy of Community law (see Chapter 6). The decision has implications for the traditional principles of parliamentary supremacy: according to the 'enrolled Act' rule, no court should be able to question the validity of statute, and under the doctrine of implied repeal, no legislation should bind a future Parliament. The *Factortame* decision means that the courts can examine the validity of legislation, in the context of whether it breaches Community law. In addition, s 2(4) of the ECA 1972 is semi-entrenched in that it extends the obligation to be consistent with Community law obligations to legislation passed in the future.

 In *R v Secretary of State for Transport, ex parte Factortame (No 5)* (1998) *The Times*, 28 April [2000] 1 AC 524 the House of Lords ruled that the UK's breach of Community law by passing the Merchant Shipping Act 1988 was sufficiently serious as to warrant the awarding of damages under the principle of State liability (see Chapter 6).

See also *R v Secretary of State for Employment, ex parte Equal Opportunities Commission* [1995] 1 AC 1.

7.3 The retention of express repeal

 Macarthys v Smith [1979] 3 All ER 32

 See **7.2.1**.

 Lord Denning
'If the time should come when our Parliament deliberately passes an Act with the intention of repudiating the Treaty or any provision in it – or intentionally of acting inconsistently with it – and says so in express terms – then I would have thought that it would be the duty of our courts to follow the statute of our Parliament.'

The retention of the ability of Parliament to expressly repeal the European Communities Act 1972 or to expressly legislate contrary to Community law is preserved according to this decision. Thus, Parliament has delegated rather than transferred supremacy to the Community. However, it is highly unlikely that Parliament would act in such a manner; expressly repealing the European Communities Act 1972 would effectively mean withdrawing from the European Union.

The comments of Lord Denning in *Macarthys* are echoed by the House of Lords in *Garland v BREL* [1982] ECR 359, particularly in the judgment of Lord Diplock:

' … having regard to the express direction as to the construction of enactments "to be passed" … contained in section 2(4), anything short of an express positive statement in an Act … that a particular provision is intended to be made in breach of [Community law] … would justify an English court in construing that provision in a manner inconsistent with a Community treaty obligation of the United Kingdom.'

As discussed in Chapter 1, there is growing recognition of the idea that there are two types of statute: ordinary statutes subject to implied repeal and constitutional statutes that may only be expressly repealed. The European Communities Act 1972 is an example of a 'constitutional statute'; see *Thoburn v Sunderland City Council* [2002] 1 CMLR 50 in Chapter 1 at **1.2**.

CHAPTER 8

CIVIL LIBERTIES

Freedom of expression
- Article 10 ECHR
R v Secretary of State for the Home Department, ex parte Brind (1991)
AG v Guardian Newspapers Ltd (No1) (1987)
R (Pro-Life Alliance) v BBC (2003)
- Contempt of court
Sunday Times v UK (1979)
Secretary of State for Defence v Guardian Newspapers Ltd (1985)
X v Morgan Grampian Ltd (1991)
- Obscenity
Shaw v DPP (1962)
Knuller v DPP (1973)

Freedom of the person
- PACE 1984
R v Longman (1988)
Christie v Leachinsky (1947)
Taylor v Thames Valley Chief Constable (2004)
O'Loughlin v Chief Constable of Essex (1998)
- Police Powers and the ECHR
Osman v DPP (1998)

Freedom of association and assembly
- Pre and Post Public Order Act 1986
Beatty v Gillbanks (1882)
DPP v Jones (1999)
- Highways Act 1980
Hirst v City Council for West Yorkshire (1986)
- Breach of the Peace
Duncan v Jones (1936); *Piddington v Bates* (1960); *Moss v McLachlan* (1985); R (Laporte) v Gloucestershire Chief Constable* (2006)

8.1 Freedom of expression

8.1.1 Art 10 ECHR

HL *R v Secretary of State for the Home Department, ex parte Brind* [1991] 1 AC 696

The Secretary of State was empowered under statute to issue directives. One directive prohibited the broadcasting of statements by representatives of proscribed organisations. The applicants were journalists seeking judicial review of the issuing of the directive, on the basis that the Secretary of State's powers should be exercised in accordance with Art 10 ECHR.

The UK courts were not bound to apply the ECHR directly until incorporated into UK law by the passing of statute. However, where there could be two interpretations of national law, one in conformity with the Convention and one not, the courts would presume that it was Parliament's intention to legislate in conformity.

Lord Bridge

' … like any other treaty obligations which have not been embodied in the law by statute, the Convention is not part of the domestic law … the courts accordingly have no power to enforce Convention rights directly and … if domestic legislation conflicts with the Convention, the courts must nevertheless enforce it'.

Because of the dualist nature of the constitution, international legal obligations, such as those stemming from treaties signed by the UK, do not

> have the force of law until incorporated by an Act
> of Parliament. (See Chapter 7 at **7.1** for
> explanation of this in the context of the EC
> Treaty.) The incorporation of the ECHR did not
> occur until the passing of the Human Rights Act
> 1998.

HL

AG v Guardian Newspapers Ltd (No 1)
[1987] 3 All ER 316 ('Spycatcher Case')

The book *Spycatcher* was written by a former member of the
intelligence services living in Australia. The book alleged that
the services had committed illegal acts. The British
Government sought to prevent publication in England and a
number of other jurisdictions, on the basis that the author was
under a duty of life-long secrecy and that the information was
confidential.

The interim injunctions imposed by the Divisional Court
were upheld by the House of Lords as being necessary in the
interests of national security and in preventing the disclosure
of confidential information.

Lord Bridge dissented (as did Lord Oliver), arguing that since
the information contained in the book was in the public
domain, there was no merit in awarding the injunctions. A
differently constituted House of Lords heard the final appeal
on the trial of the issues based on breach of confidence: *AG v
Guardian Newspapers (No 2)* [1988] 3 WLR 776. It decided to
discharge the injunctions since there had been worldwide

disclosure of the book and no further damage could be done to the public interest.

When challenged in the European Court of Human Rights (*The Observer and The Guardian v UK* (1991) 14 EHRR 153) the Court held that the period between the granting of the original injunction and the House of Lords' continuation of them had not breached Art 10 since the courts had acted proportionately given the threat to public security. However, the period between the House of Lords' continuation of the injunctions and when they were finally lifted had breached Art 10 because the confidentiality of the information no longer existed.

Tolstoy Miloslavsky v UK (1995) 20 EHRR 442.

 R (on the application of Pro-Life Alliance) v BBC
[2003] UKHL 23

The BBC refused to show an election broadcast on the basis that it was offensive. The applicants contended that this amounted to censorship and breached Art 10 ECHR.

While the Court of Appeal upheld the claim, the House of Lords disagreed; it was not unreasonable to require political parties to comply with standards of taste and decency and not be offensive.

8.1.2 Contempt of Court Act 1981

HR *Sunday Times v UK* (1979) 2 EHRR 245

In 1974 the House of Lords restored an injunction prohibiting the paper from publishing articles relating to the drug Thalidomide, which it alleged caused deformities in babies. The parents of the children intended to sue Distillers Ltd for compensation and were in protracted negotiations with them during which the common law of contempt could inhibit freedom of the press. The Sunday Times made an application, alleging that the common law of contempt violated Art 10 ECHR.

The European Court of Human Rights ruled that the ban on publication had not been proven to be necessary for maintaining the authority and impartiality of the judiciary and was consequently in breach of Art 10.

The decision in this case was very influential in the reform of the law of contempt. The Contempt of Court Act 1981 is based on strict liability, which applies under s 2 to any publications that create a 'substantial risk that the course of justice in the proceedings in question will be seriously impeded or prejudiced'. It should be noted that a modified version of the common law intentional contempt offence continues.

HL *Secretary of State for Defence v Guardian Newspapers Ltd*
[1985] AC 339

Section 10 of the Contempt of Court Act 1981 provides that a
court may not require disclosure of a source unless it is
satisfied that it is necessary in the interests of national security
or for the prevention of disorder or crime. In this case a civil
servant leaked confidential documents addressed to Ministers
and the Secretary of State for Defence to the newspaper. The
Ministry attempted to recover the documents from the
newspaper so that the identity of the person could be
established.

Section 10 could be used to prevent an action for recovery of
documents that would reveal a source. However, in this case
there was a need to recover the documents because of the
threat to national security.

HL *X v Morgan Grampian Ltd* [1991] AC 1

A confidential plan had been stolen from the plaintiffs and
information from it given to Goodwin, a journalist. The
plaintiffs applied for an order requiring the journalist to
disclose the source.

The House of Lords held that the interests of the plaintiff
outweighed those of the journalist, and ordered disclosure.

In *Goodwin v UK* (1996) 22 EHRR 123 the European Court of Human Rights criticised this decision on the basis that the protection of journalistic confidentiality was crucial to ensuring a free press, hence any interference with this protection had to be carefully scrutinised. The Court ruled that the order against the journalist had violated his right to freedom of expression.

8.1.3 Obscenity

HL | *Shaw v DPP* [1962] AC 220

Shaw had published a directory providing the names and details of prostitutes. He was prosecuted, *inter alia*, under the common law for the offence of conspiracy to corrupt public morals.

The court upheld the existence of a residual power under common law to conserve the safety and moral welfare of the State.

HL | *Knuller Ltd v DPP* [1973] AC 423

The publishers produced a magazine containing advertisements directed towards male homosexuals.

Shaw was upheld by the House of Lords, which rejected the defence that a private homosexual act between male adults was no longer an offence (Sexual Offences Act 1967).

It should be noted that the use of the common law offence of conspiracy to engage in conduct that corrupts public morals or outrage public decency is rare and few prosecutions have been brought since *Knuller*. One example was in *R v Gibson* [1990] 2 QB 619 where an art gallery and an artist were convicted after showing an exhibition which included a model's head with earrings made from a human foetus. However, the common law offence does have the advantage of not being subject to any statutory defences, as is available under the Obscene Publications Act 1959.

8.2 Freedom of the person

8.2.1 Police and Criminal Evidence Act 1984

CA *R v Longman* [1988] 1 WLR 619

Police officers, with a search warrant, entered a house through deception and only identified that they had a warrant on gaining entry.

This procedure complied with ss 15 and 16 PACE 1984; an officer was not required to identify himself or serve the search warrant before entry.

HL *Christie v Leachinsky* [1947] AC 573

The police had arrested Leachinsky, knowing that the arrest

did not comply with the necessary conditions, on which basis he sued for wrongful arrest and false imprisonment.

It is a condition of lawful arrest that the person arrested be informed of the reasons.

Section 28 of PACE 1984 now requires reasons for the arrest to be given, which must be given at the time or at some more practicable time. A lawful arrest also requires the person to be informed of the fact of arrest.

CA *Taylor v Thames Valley Chief Constable*
[2004] EWCA Civ 858

A 10-year-old boy was arrested at a demonstration and informed of the reason, violent disorder, which had taken place at a demonstration six weeks earlier.

The court offered guidelines on what constituted sufficient reasons for the purpose of lawful arrest. It was accepted that in the case at hand sufficient information had been provided.

Clarke LJ
The arrested person must be informed in 'simple, non-technical language that he could understand, the essential legal and factual grounds for his arrest'.

An officer is not required, according to this case, to provide 'detailed particulars of the case'.

Lewis v Chief Constable of South Wales [1991] 1 All ER 206

CA *O'Loughlin v Chief Constable of Essex* [1998] 1 WLR 374

The police entered the plaintiff's premises under s 17 of PACE 1984 but failed to give a reason to the occupant.

The police, when exercising statutory powers of entry by the use of reasonable force, should give the occupant present a reason.

Failure to do so in the case meant that the officers had assaulted the occupant, who was entitled to damages. This requirement can, though, be waived when it is impossible, impracticable or undesirable to do so.

8.2.2 Police powers and the ECHR

ECHR *Osman v DPP* (1998) 29 EHRR 245

A teacher formed an attachment to the applicant's son. The teacher was questioned by police after files went missing and damage was caused to the family home but no further action was taken. In 1988, the teacher shot and killed the applicant's husband and the deputy headmaster's son and shot and injured the applicant's son and deputy headmaster. Civil action against the police was struck out in the Court of Appeal in 1992 on the basis that the police were immune from civil actions for public policy reasons. The applicant contended there had been violations of Arts 2, 6 and 8 of the Convention.

The European Court of Human Rights found no breach in respect of Arts 2 and 8 but did conclude that the inability to take civil action against the police was contrary to Art 6 (right to a fair trial) in that it was a disproportionate restriction on the applicant's right of access to a court.

The European Court has since identified that it had misunderstood the English law: see *Z v UK* (2002) 34 EHRR 245.

In *Brogan v UK* (1988) 11 EHRR 117 the ECHR held that detention of up to seven days at the Home Secretary's discretion was contrary to Art 5 (right to liberty).

In *Price v UK* (2001) *The Times*, 13 August, the Court ruled that the conditions of detention in both a police station and prison for a severely disabled person violated Art 3 (freedom from torture, inhuman and degrading treatment).

In *Edwards v UK* (2002) *The Times*, 1 April the Court examined the death of a prisoner killed by a schizophrenic inmate that had a history of violence. The Court ruled that there had been violation of Art 2 (the right to life); Art 1 in that there had been no effective investigation; and Art 13 (remedies) in that the victim's parents could not secure compensation.

8.3 Freedom of association and assembly

8.3.1 Assembly pre-Public Order Act 1986

 CA *Beatty v Gillbanks* (1882) 9 QBD 308

The Salvation Army had held processions that had been violently opposed. The magistrates' court issued an order preventing a meeting but one was held regardless. The police ordered the meeting to disband and arrested one of the members.

The court held that there had been no unlawful assembly.

Unlawful assembly has since been abolished and replaced by s 2 of the Public Order Act 1986. In contrast, in *Jordan v Burgoyne* [1963] 2 QB 744 it was held that a person addressing an audience with words likely to inflame and lead to violence would be guilty of breach of the peace (see below).

8.3.2 Post-Public Order Act 1986

 HL *DPP v Jones* [1999] 2 AC 240

An order under s 14A of the Public Order Act 1986 had been issued, prohibiting the holding of a 'trespassory assembly' within a 4-mile radius of Stonehenge. The assembly was within the 4-mile radius and on the public highway but it was peaceful. The protestors present refused to disperse and were arrested and convicted of trespassory assembly.

The decision of the Crown Court to overturn the conviction was reinstated by the House of Lords. The right to use the highway in this way meant that there was no trespass under the Public Order Act 1986.

' ... the public highway is a public place which the public may enjoy for any reasonable purpose, provided the activity in question does not amount to a public or private nuisance and does not obstruct the highway by unreasonably impeding the primary right of the public to pass and repass; within these qualifications there is a public right of peaceful assembly on the highway'.

In *Flockhart v Robinson* [1950] 2 KB 498 a procession was defined as 'a body of persons moving along a route'.

8.3.3 Highways Act 1980

DC **Hirst v City Council for West Yorkshire** (1986) 85 Cr App R 143

Section 137 of the Highways Act 1980 states that it is an offence wilfully to obstruct free passage along a highway. In this case, animal rights demonstrators protesting outside a shop selling animal fur were charged with obstructing the highway. The magistrates' court convicted them of obstruction.

A court must examine the reasonableness of the action,

balancing the right to demonstrate with the need to protect public order, which the magistrates' court had failed to do.

In *DPP v Jones* (1999) (see **8.3.2**) the House of Lords stated that it could be lawful to use the highway for the purpose of demonstrating. It is a matter of fact as to whether in each case the use is reasonable. See, in contrast, *Hubbard v Pitt* [1976] QB 142.

8.3.4 Breach of the peace

 Duncan v Jones [1936] 1 KB 218

Duncan refused to move a meeting she intended to hold on the highway where previous disturbances had occurred. She was arrested and charged with obstructing the police.

If a police officer reasonably believes that a breach of the peace will occur, he may attempt to prevent it and any action that impedes him from doing so amounts to obstruction of a police officer in the execution of his duty.

The decision has been criticised on the basis that it extends too much power to the police in controlling meetings etc.

 Piddington v Bates [1960] 3 All ER 660

The appellant was arrested after joining a picket when a police officer had instructed that only two persons be present at each picket.

A police officer has the power to restrict numbers demonstrating or picketing.

Lord Parker CJ
' ... a police officer charged with the duty of preserving the Queen's peace must be left to take such steps as, on the evidence before him, he thinks are proper'.

The police thus have wide discretionary powers under the common law to prevent breach of the peace (and, by implication, arrest for obstruction of a police officer). As identified above, the police have the power to give directions as to how a demonstration can be conducted, including dispersal. The extent of these powers is clearly seen in the next case.

DC *Moss v McLachlan* [1985] IRLR 76

Breach of the peace traditionally required a degree of proximity and immediacy. In this case, during the miners' strike, the defendants were ordered to turn back on a journey to another picket line four miles away, on the basis that the police believed there would be a breach of the peace. The miners refused and were arrested for obstruction.

A police officer that 'honestly and reasonably' believes that there is a real risk of a breach of the peace in an area proximate to the point of arrest can take whatever measures necessary to prevent it.

In *R v Howell* [1982] QB 416 it was established that a common law power of arrest would exist when the breach of peace was committed in the presence of the person making the arrest; or if they reasonably believed the breach would occur in the immediate future; or if the breach had already occurred and it was reasonably believed that it would happen again.

A breach of the peace itself has been defined in *Bibby v Chief Constable of Essex* (2000) *The Times*, 24 April as an unreasonable, 'sufficiently real and present threat' that comes from the person to be arrested and which clearly interferes with the rights of others.

 ### R (Laporte) v Gloucestershire Chief Constable
[2006] UKHL 55

A coach carrying anti-Iraq war protestors travelling to a demonstration was stopped and searched by the police some miles from the demonstration site. The coach was then turned back with a police escort. The police claimed that their powers extended to taking action whenever they reasonably anticipated that a breach of the peace was likely.

The House of Lords, in reviewing the police common law powers to prevent a breach of the peace, emphasised the importance of freedom of expression and noted the increased level of legislative constraint on the public's ability to protest. It held that the common law power to prevent a breach of the peace was confined to a situation where the breach was actually taking place or was imminent.

The House of Lords was critical of the decision in *Piddington* (above). The court recognised that the police had to have some discretion and Lord Bingham considered the decision in *Moss* (above), where demonstrators were also turned back, to be an example of where there was a borderline threat of an imminent breach of the peace. In this case the court concluded that the police had acted disproportionately, since freedom of expression should only be limited as a last resort.

CHAPTER 9

HUMAN RIGHTS

ECHR (examples of cases involving Arts 2, 3, 5, 6 and 8)

Art 2   *McCann, Farrell and Savage v UK* (1995)
Art 3   *Ireland v UK* (1978) and *Chahal v UK* (1997)
Art 5   *Brogan v UK* (1988)
Art 6   *T and V v UK* [1999]
Art 8   *Malone v UK* (1984); *Halford v UK* (1997); *Dudgeon v UK* (1982)

HUMAN RIGHTS ACT 1998

- **s 3: the extent of the interpretative duty**

Ghaidan v Codin-Mendoza (2004): s 3 should be attempted before recourse to s 4
R v A (Complainant's Sexual History) (2001): the extent of the obligation to interpret
Re W and B (Children: Care Plan) (2002): the need to reserve the distinction between interpretation and redrafting statute

- **s 4: issuing declarations of incompatibility**

R (on the application of Alconbury Developments Ltd) v Secretary of State for the Environment, Transport and the Regions and other cases (2001): example of declaration being overturned
R (H) v London North and East Region Mental Health Review Tribunal (2001): example of declaration being issued

- **s 6: public authorities**

Billesley Parochial Church Council v Wallbank (2001) and *YL v Birmingham City Council and others* (2007): examples of what constitutes a public authority

9.1 The ECHR: examples of cases invoking substantive rights

9.1.1 Article 2

 CHR *McCann, Farrell and Savage v UK* (1995) 21 EHRR 97

Article 2 guarantees the right to life. There is, though, no violation of the provision if loss of life is caused by reasonable self-defence against unlawful violence, to carry out a lawful arrest or to stop/prevent civil unrest. The killing of three Irish Republican Army members in Gibraltar by the SAS was challenged as being in breach of this Article.

The action taken must be proportionate to the particular circumstances of the case. The security forces had information establishing that there was a threat but the actual killing of the persons was 'more than absolutely necessary' as provided within Art 2.

According to *R (on the application of Pretty) v DPP* (2001) *The Times*, 5 December (and *Pretty v UK* (2002) 35 EHRR 1) Art 2 cannot be interpreted so as to establish a right to voluntary euthanasia. In the case the court emphasised that the Convention is intended only to protect widely shared values – it is not designed to intervene in moral issues where there is no consensus.

See also *Jordan v UK* (2003) 37 EHRR 52.

9.1.2 Article 3

 Ireland v UK (1978) 2 EHRR 25

Article 3 of the Convention states that no-one shall be subjected to torture, degrading or inhuman treatment or punishment. In 1971 the Government introduced powers of detention and internment for suspected IRA terrorists. Practices such as hooding, sleep deprivation, and withholding of food and water were alleged.

The treatment was concluded to be inhuman and/or degrading treatment within the terms of Art 3.

The treatment was not considered to amount to torture because it did not result in the required intensity of suffering/cruelty.

 Chahal v UK (1997) 23 EHRR 413

A Sikh and political activist who, on a previous visit to India, had been tortured, was threatened with deportation to India on grounds of national security.

The treatment was concluded to be inhuman and/or degrading treatment within the terms of Art 3.

Returning a person to their country of origin when they are likely to face torture or degrading, inhuman treatment will breach Art 3.

In *D v UK* (1997) 24 EHRR 423, D was threatened with deportation to his home country on the basis that he was an illegal immigrant and convicted criminal. He was terminally ill and there was no-one in his home country that could care for him. The ECrtHR concluded that this was a breach of Art 3.

In *A v Secretary of State for the Home Department (No 2)* [2005] 3 WLR 1249, it was concluded that evidence obtained by torture in another country cannot be used in the English courts.

See also *East African Asians v UK* (1973) 3 EHRR 76 and *Tyrer v UK* (1978) 2 EHRR 1.

9.1.3 Article 5

 CHR *Brogan v UK* (1988) 11 EHRR 117

The Prevention of Terrorism (Temporary Provisions) Act 1974 permitted the Home Secretary the discretion to detain for up to seven days.

This was a violation of Art 5, which provides that everyone has the right to liberty and security of person and that no-one can be deprived of their liberty other than in accordance with the law.

However, the Government responded by depositing a limited derogation from the Convention, declaring the power necessary on the grounds of national security.

Failure to bring an arrested person before a judge in a prompt and timely manner breaches Art 5: *O'Hara v UK* (2001) *The Times*, 13 November. In *Caballero v UK* (2000) 30 EHRR 643 it was held that the automatic denial of bail for some offences in the Criminal Justice and Public Order Act 1994 breached Art 5. See also, for example, *L v UK* (2004) *The Times*, 19 October; *Oldham v UK* (2001) 31 EHRR 34; *Murray v UK* (1996) 22 EHRR 29.

9.1.4 Article 6

 T and V v UK [1999] *The Times*, 17 December

Juveniles convicted of murder had their tariff period set by the Home Secretary on the basis of retribution and deterrence. The juveniles in question had also been tried in an adult court.

Trying juveniles in an adult court violated Art 6 in that it was not a fair trial. In addition, the setting of the tariff by the Home Secretary deprived them of seeking review of the detention period by a judicial body.

In *Steel and Morris v UK* (2005) 41 EHRR 403 two activists were denied legal aid to defend themselves in an action for libel brought by McDonald's. This was concluded to be a breach of Art 6.

See also *Brennan v UK* (2001) *The Times*, 22 October; *Benham v UK* (1996) 22 EHRR 293; *McGonnell v UK* (2000) 30 EHRR 289; *Saunders v UK* (1997) 23 EHRR 313; and *Osman v DPP* (1998) 29 EHRR 245 in Chapter 8.

9.1.5 Article 8

 Malone v UK (1984) 7 EHRR 14

Malone challenged the UK Government's tapping of his telephone as a breach of Art 8 – the right to respect for private and family life, home and correspondence.

The practices adopted by the UK Government were too unclear and in breach of Art 8.

ECHR

' ... it cannot be said with any reasonable certainty what elements of the powers to intercept are incorporated in legal rules and what elements remain within the discretion of the executive ... the law ... does not indicate with reasonable clarity the scope and manner of exercise of the relevant discretion ... To that extent the minimum degree of legal protection to which citizens are entitled under the rule of law in a democratic society is lacking'.

As a result, the Government introduced the Interception of Communications Act 1985 ensuring statutory basis for the granting of warrants authorising interception of communications.

ECHR *Halford v UK* (1997) 24 EHRR 523

Halford was an Assistant Chief Constable. She discovered that her work telephone calls had been intercepted by senior police officers.

The Court did not accept the defence that the phones were intercepted lawfully because they were government property and concluded there had been a breach of Art 8.

See also *Roche v UK* (2005) *The Times,* 27 October.

 ECHR *Dudgeon v UK* (1982) 4 EHRR 149

Legislation in Northern Ireland prohibited homosexual acts between male adults.

There was a violation of Art 8 in respect of the right to respect for a private sexual life.

The law was changed by the Homosexual Offences (Northern Ireland) Order 1982.

In *Lustig-Prean and Beckett v UK* (2000) 29 EHRR 548 the Court ruled that a ban on homosexuals in the armed forces was a breach of Art 8. See also *ADT v UK* (2000) 2 FLR 697 and *Smith v UK* (2000) 29 EHRR 493.

CA *Douglas v Hello! Ltd* [2001] QB 967

The claimants had entered into a contract with a magazine to publish their wedding photographs. They requested an injunction to prevent a rival magazine from publishing unauthorised pictures.

The law extended to preventing publication of material taken in breach of confidence. The Court rejected the claim for an injunction – according to the facts, the wedding had not been private, so there was no duty of confidentiality.

Brooke LJ

' … equity may intervene to prevent the publication of photographic images taken in breach of an obligation of confidence'.

The courts have not responded to Art 8 of the Convention by deciding to create a new tort of privacy but by developing the law of breach of confidence.

Venables v News Group Newspapers Ltd [2001] Fam 430; *Campbell v MGN Ltd* [2004] UKHL 22.

9.1.6 Article 10

See Chapter 8.

9.2 Human Rights Act 1998

9.2.1 The status of the ECHR pre-Human Rights Act

 R v Secretary of State for the Home Department, ex parte Brind [1991] 1 AC 696

See Chapter 8 at **8.1**.

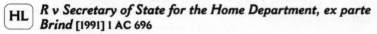

In *Attorney-General v BBC* [1981] AC 303 and *Attorney-General v Guardian Newspapers (No 2)* [1990] 1 AC 109 the House of Lords confirmed that the courts were under a duty to interpret national law in light of the obligations under the Convention. This included both legislation (*Waddington v Miah* [1974] 1 WLR 683) and common law (*Derbyshire County Council v Times Newspapers Ltd* [1993] AC 534).

9.2.2 Section 3

 HL *Ghaidan v Godin-Mendoza* [2004] UKHL 30

 The Rent Act 1977 provided that on the death of a protected tenant their spouse, if then living in the house, became a tenant by succession. In a previous case the House of Lords had ruled that this did not extend to same-sex relationships. This was challenged in this case.

 The House of Lords used s 3 to reinterpret the statute so that it was compatible with the Convention, extending the rights to same-sex relationships, rather than issue a s 4 declaration of incompatibility.

 Lord Steyn
' ... interpretation under section 3(1) is the prime remedial remedy and ... resort to section 4 must always be an exceptional course'.

➤ In *Wilson v First County Trust (No 2)* [2003] 3 WLR 568 the House of Lords concluded that there is no power to grant a declaration on incompatibility under s 4 (see below) unless the interpretative duty under s 3 had first been attempted.

 HL *R v A (Complainant's Sexual History)* (2001) *The Times*, 24 May

It was contended that statutory restrictions under the Criminal Evidence Act 1999 on the admissibility of evidence prejudiced the right to a fair trial.

A court is obligated under s 3 to find an interpretation
compatible with the ECHR. The court could therefore
construe the Act so as to permit the necessary evidence to
ensure a fair trial since this was the general purpose of the
statute.

Lord Steyn
Section 3 'went further than requiring the court to take the
Convention into account: the court had a duty to strive to
find a possible interpretation compatible with Convention
rights'.

Thus, the courts may, as Lord Steyn noted, have to 'adopt an
interpretation which may appear linguistically strained'.
However, there must be a distinction between legitimate
interpretation and stepping into the realm of redrafting
legislation.

HL *Re W and B (Children: Care Plan)*
[2002] *The Times*, 15 March

The Children Act 1989 was interpreted by the
Court of Appeal so that it required authorities to
implement care plans within time limits, although
no such provision had been made by Parliament.

On appeal, the House of Lords concluded that the
Court of Appeal's interpretation went beyond the
scope of s 3. A constitutional boundary has to be
maintained between the legislative supremacy of
Parliament in drafting and amending statute and

the role played by the courts in interpreting statute.

There is therefore a notion of judicial deference, and this can be witnessed in, for example, *R v DPP, ex parte Kebeline and Others* [1999] 3 WLR 175, where Lord Hope stated that in certain circumstances it would be appropriate for the courts 'to recognise that there is an area of judgment within which the judiciary defer, on democratic grounds, to the considered opinion of the elected body'. Similarly, in *R v Lambert, Ali and Jordan* [2001] 1 All ER 1014 Lord Woolf stated that 'legislation is passed by a democratically elected Parliament and therefore the courts ... are entitled to and should, as a matter of constitutional principle, pay a degree of deference to the view of Parliament ... '.

In *R (Carson) v Works and Pensions Secretary* [2005] UKHL 37 the court held that the Government did not have to justify treating pensioners resident overseas less favourably than those residing in the UK, since that was considered by Parliament to be fair.

Bellinger v Bellinger [2003] 2 All ER 593; *Cachia v Faluyi* [2002] 1 All ER 192.

9.2.3 Declarations of incompatibility

HL *R (on the application of Alconbury Developments Ltd) v Secretary of State for the Environment, Transport and the Regions and other cases* [2001] UKHL 23

In respect of four planning cases, the Divisional Court had issued a declaration of incompatibility in respect of the Secretary of State's decision-making powers as being in breach of Art 6.

The House of Lords quashed the declaration on the basis that if the Secretary of State did not act impartially when hearing appeals, his decision would be subject to judicial review and this was a sufficient remedy.

Some declarations of incompatibility have been upheld and promoted legislative reform. However, as in this case, whilst the High Court has been prepared to issue them, a number have been overturned on appeal. In *Wilson v First County Trust (No 2)* [2003] 3 WLR 568 it was held that the power to issue a declaration of incompatibility only exists where the duty of interpretation is applicable and this cannot be the case when the facts of the case took place before the Human Rights Act came into force.

For Key Cases on judicial review, see Chapters 10 and 11.

CA *R (H) v London North and East Region Mental Health Review Tribunal* [2001] EWCA Civ 415

A patient could apply to a mental health review tribunal for discharge from detention in hospital but, under statute, the patient faced the burden of proof of establishing that at least one of the criteria for their continued detention was no longer satisfied.

The Court of Appeal held that this breached Art 5; the burden of proof should have rested on those detaining the patient. The court was not able to interpret the statutory provisions to ensure compliance so issued a declaration of incompatibility.

See *International Transport Roth GmbH v Secretary of State for the Home Department* [2002] EWCA Civ 158 for an additional example of the Court of Appeal issuing a declaration of incompatibility.

9.2.4 Section 6

HL *Aston Cantlow and Wilmcote with Billesley Parochial Church Council v Wallbank* [2003] UKHL 37

The Council had statutory duties to enforce church repairs but it had to be established whether it was a public authority for the purposes of s 6 of the Human Rights Act 1998.

The Council was not a public authority on the basis that the Church of England was not a core public authority.

Lord Nicholls
'Factors to be taken into account include the extent to which in carrying out the relevant functions the body is publicly funded, or is exercising statutory powers, or is taking the place of central government or local authorities, or is providing a public service.'

In contrast, in *Poplar Housing and Regeneration Community Association Ltd v Donoghue* [2001] EWCA Civ 595 a housing association performing functions similar to that of a local authority was considered a public authority.

 HL | *YL v Birmingham City Council and others* [2007] UKHL 27

The claimant, aged 84, suffered from Alzheimer's disease. Since January 2006 she had lived in a privately owned, profit-earning care home. The defendant local authority arranged and largely funded the placement. In June 2006, after a number of problems, the care home decided to give the claimant 28 days notice. The Official Solicitor launched proceedings on the claimant's behalf in the Family Division seeking a declaration, *inter alia*, that the care home, in providing accommodation and care for the claimant, was exercising public functions for the purpose of s 6 of the Human Rights Act 1998. That issue was decided against the

claimant, and her appeal was dismissed by the Court of
Appeal. She appealed against that decision.

The House of Lords dismissed the appeal; the care home was
not exercising functions of a public nature within the meaning
of s 6(3)(b) of the Human Rights Act 1998. The provision of
care and accomodation for those unable to arrange it
themselves was not an inherently governmental function; the
care home acted as a private, profit-earning company.

CHAPTER 10

JUDICIAL REVIEW
JURISDICTION AND PROCEDURE

Procedure of application

O'Reilly v Mackman (1983)
public vs private matters

↓

Definition of a 'public body'

R v Panel on Takeovers and Mergers, ex parte Datafin (1987)
body performing governmental functions
R v Disciplinary Committee of the Jockey Club, ex parte Aga Khan
(1993)
R (on the application of Julian West) v Lloyd's of London (2004)

↓

Sufficient interest

R v IRC, ex parte National Federation of Self-employed and Small
Businesses (1982)
determined in two stages
R v Secretary of State for the Environment, ex parte Rose Theatre
Trust Co Ltd (1990)
pressure groups and *locus standi*
R v Secretary of State for the Environment, ex parte Greenpeace Ltd
(No 2) (1994)
pressure groups and *locus standi*

↓

Exclusion of judicial review

Anisminic v Foreign Compensation Commission (1969)
complete ouster clauses ineffective

10.1 Procedure of application for judicial review

HL *O'Reilly v Mackman* [1983] 2 AC 237

Four prisoners alleged by writ and summons that a prison had acted contrary to certain rules. The defendants applied to have the action struck out as an abuse of process, arguing that such action should only proceed by way of judicial review.

As a general rule, actions by a public body affecting public law matters should be commenced by way of judicial review.

In the 1970s there had been demands for reform of the remedies available in administrative law. In 1977 a new Rule of the Supreme Court (Ord 53) created the procedure for applying for judicial review, which was confirmed by Parliament in s 31 Supreme Court Act 1981. This decision utilises the reforms by emphasising that for most cases in public law proceeding for judicial review is the appropriate remedy. In 2000, RSC Ord 53 was replaced by Pt 54 of the Civil Procedure Rules.

The *O'Reilly* case generated the concept that judicial review would be the exclusive procedure in public law cases. However, this caused problems in that much time was spent in litigation trying to determine whether the correct procedure had been used. However, it is no longer the case that the procedure for judicial review is exclusively used: see, for example, *Roy v Kensington Family Practitioner Committee*

[1992] 1 AC 624 and *Mercury Communications plc v Customs and Excise Commissioners* [1997] 2 All ER 366.

10.2 Definition of a 'public body'

 CA *R v Panel on Takeovers and Mergers, ex parte Datafin* [1987] QB 815

 Judicial review is only available against public bodies. If the body whose decision is being challenged is considered a private body, the remedy will lie in private law. The applicants sought judicial review of the Panel's rejection of their complaint. The Panel contended that its actions were not subject to judicial review because it was not a public body; its powers did not derive from statute or prerogative.

 The Panel was a public body because it was performing public functions that would otherwise be performed by government.

 Lloyd LJ
' … if a body in question is exercising public law functions, or if the exercise of its functions have public law consequences, then that may be sufficient to bring the body within the reach of judicial review'.

 CA *R v Disciplinary Committee of the Jockey Club, ex parte Aga Khan* [1993] 1 WLR 909

The Aga Khan sought judicial review of the decision of the Jockey Club to disqualify his horse.

The decision was subject to much academic criticism on the basis that it potentially prevented pressure groups from seeking judicial review. However, a year later, in *R v Poole Borough Council, ex parte BeeBee* [1991] 2 PLR 27 a different conclusion was reached when two pressure groups were recognised as having the necessary *locus standi*. This more liberal approach can also be seen in the following case.

DC | ***R v Secretary of State for the Environment, ex parte Greenpeace Ltd (No 2)*** [1994] 4 All ER 352

 Greenpeace applied for judicial review of the decision of the Inspectorate of Pollution to allow a nuclear processing plant to be built.

 The court declined to follow *Rose Theatre*. Whether a pressure group has the necessary sufficient interest must be examined in the context of the facts of the case. In this case Greenpeace had sufficient interest (although the application for review failed because the Minister had acted lawfully).

 Greenpeace was concluded to have *locus standi* because of its nature as a large organisation with the prime objective of protecting the environment. In addition, it had a considerable number of members residing within the affected area. It was therefore in the public interest to permit Greenpeace to bring the action.

 In *R v Secretary of State for Foreign and Commonwealth Affairs, ex parte World Development Movement* [1995] 1 All ER 611 the WDM was concluded to have sufficient interest because it played a significant role in giving advice and assistance in relation to the granting of foreign aid and because it would be unlikely that any other body would have the necessary interest, ie it was the public interest to grant the WDM *locus standi.*

See also *R v Secretary of State for Employment, ex parte Equal Opportunities Commission and Another* [1995] 1 AC 1.

10.4 Attempts to exclude judicial review completely

 HL | ***Anisminic v Foreign Compensation Commission***
[1969] 2 AC 147

 Anisminic's claim to the Foreign Compensation Commission failed. The Foreign Compensation Act 1950, s 4(4) stated that no decisions of the FCC 'could be called in question in any court of law' (an ouster clause).

 The House of Lords held that the jurisdiction of the courts could not be ousted – if a decision has been made *ultra vires* (without jurisdiction) it is not a decision, and therefore the court retains the jurisdiction to examine it under judicial review. The court concluded that the FCC had misunderstood its legal powers when making its decision and the courts could therefore intervene.

 Lord Wilberforce
'What would be the purpose of defining by statute the limits of a tribunal's powers, if by means of a

clause inserted in the instrument … those limits could safely be passed?'

This important judgment effectively renders complete ouster clauses ineffective. It also protects the operation of the rule of law (see Chapter 2).

R v Hull University Visitor, ex parte Page [1993] AC 682.

CHAPTER 11

JUDICIAL REVIEW: THE GROUNDS

The GCHQ Case (1985)

Illegality

Narrow ultra vires	*AG v Fulham Corporation* (1921)
Error of law	*Perilly v Tower Hamlets BC* (1973)
	R v Home Secretary, ex parte Venables (1998)
Error of fact	*R v Home Secretary, ex parte Khawaja* (1984)
Improper purpose	*R v Foreign Secretary, ex parte WDM* (1995)
	Congreve v Home Office (1976)
	Porter v Magill (2001)
Relevant/ irrelevant considerations	*Bromley LBC v GLC* (1983)
	R v Home Secretary, ex parte Venables (1998)
Unauthorised delegation	*Carltona v Works Commissioners* (1943)
Fettering discretion	*Sagnata v Norwich Corporation* (1971)
	BOC v Board of Trade (1971)

Irrationality/Unreasonableness

Unreasonableness	*Associated Picture Houses v Wednesbury Corp* (1948)
Unreasonable conditions	*Pyx Granite v Minister of Housing & Local Government* (1958)
Proportionality	*R v Home Secretary, ex parte Brind* (1991)
	R (Daly) v Home Secretary (2001)

Procedural impropriety

Statutory rules	*Bradbury v Enfield* (1967)
	Ridge v Baldwin (1964)
Right to hearing	*Ridge v Baldwin* (1964)
Reasons	*R v Home Secretary, ex parte Doody* (1993)
Rule against bias	*Dimes v Grand Junction Canal* (1852)
	R v Bow Street Magistrates' Court, ex parte Pinochet (No 2) (1999)
	Porter v Magill (2002)
Legitimate expectation	*AG for HK v Ng Yuen Shiu* (1983)

11.1 The GCHQ case – the three grounds

HL *Council of Civil Service Unions v Minister of State for the Civil Service* [1985] AC 374 (GCHQ Case)

See Chapter 5 at **5.2.4**.

In the context of judicial review, the House of Lords summarised the three grounds for review as being illegality, irrationality and procedural impropriety.

Lord Diplock
'Judicial review has I think developed to a state today when ... one can conveniently classify under three heads the grounds on which administrative action is subject to control by judicial review. The first ground I would call "illegality", the second "irrationality" and the third "procedural impropriety"'

'By "illegality" ... I mean that the decision maker must understand correctly the law that regulates his decision making power and give effect to it.'

'By "irrationality", I mean what can now be succinctly referred to as *Wednesbury* unreasonableness. It applies to a decision which is so outrageous in its defiance of logic or of accepted moral standards that no sensible person who had applied his mind to the question to be decided could have arrived at it.'

'I have described the third head as "procedural impropriety" rather than failure to observe basic rules of natural justice or failure to act with

> procedural fairness ... This is because
> susceptibility to judicial review under this head
> covers also failure by an administrative tribunal to
> observe the procedural rules that are expressly laid
> down in the legislative instrument by which its
> jurisdiction is conferred.'

 Lord Diplock also recognised that further grounds
could be accepted in the future, referring
particularly to the concept of proportionality (see
below).

11.2 Illegality

11.2.1 Narrow *ultra vires*

Example: *AG v Fulham Corporation* [1921] 1 Ch 440

A local authority had power to provide a non-commercial
'wash house' for local people. The authority interpreted this as
authorising the provision of a commercial laundry service.

The court interpreted 'wash house' to mean a place where
people would do their own laundry, not a laundry service
where it was done by staff. Hence, the local authority had
acted illegally.

11.2.2 Error of law

Example: *Perilly v Tower Hamlets Borough Council*
[1973] QB 9

A local authority believed that it had to consider applications
for stall licences in the order in which they were received.
Perilly was denied a licence even though his deceased mother
had held one for 30 years.

The local authority had misinterpreted the law.

*R v Monopolies and Mergers Commission, ex parte South
Yorkshire Transport Ltd* [1993] 1 All ER 289.

Example: *R v Secretary of State for the Home Department,
ex parte Venables* **[1998] AC 407**

The Home Secretary increased the tariff period for two young
murderers to 15 years, on the basis that they should be treated
in the same way as adults.

The Home Secretary had misdirected himself as to the law,
rendering the decision unlawful.

Lord Steyn
'His legal premise was wrong: the two sentences are different.
A sentence of detention during Her Majesty's pleasure requires

the Home Secretary to decide from time to time ... whether detention is still justified. The Home Secretary misunderstood his duty. This misdirection by itself renders his decision unlawful.'

R v Somerset County Council, ex parte Fewings [1995] 3 All ER 20.

11.2.3 Error of fact

Example: *R v Secretary of State for the Home Department, ex parte Khawaja* **[1984] AC 74**

Under the Immigration Act 1971 the Home Secretary could deport 'illegal immigrants'. It was contended that the standard of proof to be applied was whether there were reasonable grounds for the decision.

The House of Lords held that an illegal immigrant included one that entered through fraud or deception (this fact had to be established before any power to detain could be exercised). In such cases the standard of proof that deception had occurred had to be one of a high degree of probability.

11.2.4 Acting for an improper purpose

Example: *R v Secretary of State for Foreign and Commonwealth Affairs, ex parte World Development Movement* **[1995] 1 All ER 611**

In 1988 the UK Government agreed to sell arms to Malaysia.

In 1989 the UK offered £234 million towards the building of the Pergau Dam. (Linking arms with aid is prohibited under international law.) Section 1 of the Overseas Development and Co-operation Act 1980 empowers the Foreign Secretary to grant aid 'only for the purpose of promoting the development or maintaining the economy of a country … or the welfare of its people'.

The High Court held that the Foreign Secretary had acted unlawfully in that the aid did not promote the development of the country's economy.

Example: *Congreve v Home Office* [1976] QB 629

The Home Office told some people holding television licences that they would have to pay an extra amount or the licence would be revoked by the Home Secretary.

The Court of Appeal held this to be an improper exercise of the Home Secretary's powers.

Example: *Porter v Magill* [2001] UKHL 673

Westminster Council, which had a Conservative majority, had decided to adopt a policy of selling council houses in parts of the city, believing that those home owners would vote Conservative.

The House of Lords held that this was improper use of the Council's powers.

11.2.5 Relevant and irrelevant considerations

Example: *Bromley London Borough Council v Greater London Council* **[1983] 1 AC 768**

The GLC wanted to reduce traffic congestion and increase the numbers on public transport, so sought to increase rates to subsidise London Transport.

The House of Lords held that reducing traffic congestion was an irrelevant consideration. In contrast, the failure to consider the interests of ratepayers amounted to a failure to take into account relevant considerations. The GLC had the power to raise funds to subsidise transport but this had to be based on ordinary business principles.

See also *Wheeler v Leicester City Council* [1985] AC 1054; *R v Liverpool Crown Court, ex parte Luxury Leisure Ltd* (1998) *The Times,* 26 October

Example: *R v Secretary of State for the Home Department, ex parte Venables* **[1998] AC 407**

See above. In making the decision to increase the tariff the Home Secretary had considered public petitions demanding life sentences.

The Home Secretary had considered irrelevant considerations (the public petitions) and failed to consider relevant considerations (the progress and development of the children while in detention).

11.2.6 Unauthorised delegation

Example: *Carltona v Works Commissioners*
[1943] 2 All ER 560

Under wartime regulations Carltona's property was requisitioned, but the order was signed by a civil servant.

A Minister may lawfully delegate power but remains accountable to Parliament for any decision.

See Chapter 5. In contrast, in *R v Talbot Borough Council, ex parte Jones* [1988] 2 All ER 207 it was held that a decision to grant local authority housing had been unlawfully sub-delegated from the chairman and vice-chairman of the appropriate committee to a housing officer. Similarly, in *Barnard v National Dock Labour Board* [1953] 2 QB 18 the Board lawfully delegated disciplinary functions to local boards but one local board then unlawfully sub-delegated the functions to the port manager.

11.2.7 Fettering discretion

Example: *Sagnata Investments v Norwich Corporation* **[1971] 2 QB 614**

The corporation had adopted a policy not to grant any licences for amusement arcades in Norwich.

The corporation had fettered its discretion to the point where it paid no regard at all to the merits of each case.

See also *R v Secretary of State for the Home Department, ex parte Simms* [1999] 3 WLR 328 in which a blanket policy adopted by the Home Secretary preventing professionals visiting prisoners (eg journalists) was held to be unlawful.

Example: *British Oxygen Co v Board of Trade* [1971] AC 610

A scheme provided for discretionary grants to industries. The Board of Trade adopted a policy of not paying for items costing less than £25. BOC sought to challenge the Board's decision to refuse a grant for gas cylinders costing £20 each (BOC had spent over £4 million in total).

Policies or rules may be adopted but they must not be applied in a blanket manner or as automatically binding; discretion to discuss the merits of each case must be available.

11.3 Irrationality/unreasonableness

11.3.1 *Wednesbury* unreasonableness

CA | ***Associated Provincial Picture Houses v Wednesbury Corporation* [1948] 1 KB 223**

 The court had to consider the legality of a condition imposed under statute. The statute permitted 'such conditions as the authority think fit to impose'. In this case the condition was that no children under the age of 15 could be admitted to the cinema on a Sunday.

 The condition was not unreasonable.

 Lord Greene MR
A court may set aside a decision for unreasonableness only when the authority has come to a conclusion 'so unreasonable that no reasonable authority could ever have come to it'.

 In the *GCHQ case* (see **11.1**) Lord Diplock stated that the courts would only apply this ground when the decision has no rational basis or 'is so outrageous in its denial of accepted moral standards that no sensible person who has applied his mind to the question … could have arrived at it'.

 Many have criticised the *Wednesbury* test as too difficult to meet when challenging Executive discretion and have argued that there should be adoption of the European concept of 'proportionality'. (See below.)

11.3.2 Unreasonable conditions

 Pyx Granite Co Ltd v Minister of Housing and Local Government [1958] 1 QB 554

Planning permission was conditional upon the company constructing a road at its own expense when required to by the local authority and granting a public right of way over it.

A decision may be unreasonable if conditions that are difficult or impossible to perform are attached to it.

R v Hillingdon LBC, ex parte Royco Homes Ltd [1974] QB 720.

11.3.3 Proportionality

 R v Secretary of State for the Home Department, ex parte Brind [1991] 1 AC 696

Judicial review was sought of two directives issued by the Home Secretary banning transmission of speech by representatives of the IRA and Sinn Fein.

The Home Secretary had not exercised his power under the Broadcasting Act 1981 in an unreasonable manner. The concept of proportionality found in European law could not be applied without incorporation of the ECHR.

The Human Rights Act 1998 incorporated the ECHR (see Chapter 9). The next case was heard after the Act had come into force.

HL | *R (on the application of Daly) v Secretary of State for the Home Department* [2001] 2 AC 532

 Judicial review was sought of the policy of removing prisoners from their cells during searches, which included looking at their legal correspondence.

 The policy was unlawful under both common law principles and Art 8 ECHR.

 It was observed by Lord Steyn that proportionality would require a more intense examination of the action taken than review under the concept of *Wednesbury* unreasonableness.

 In *R (Alconbury Developments Ltd) v Secretary of State for the Environment, Transport and the Regions* [2001] UKHL 23 Lord Slynn stated that 'even without reference to the Human Rights Act the time has come to recognise that this principle [proportionality] is part of English law ... '.

Similarly, in *R (ABCIER) v Secretary of Sate for Defence* [2002] EWCA Civ 473 Lord Slynn argued that proportionality should be recognised in English law.

11.4 Procedural impropriety

11.4.1 Statutory rules of procedure

Bradbury v Enfield LBC [1967] 1 WLR 1311

The Education Act 1944 provided that a local authority wishing to close schools or create new ones had to consult the public.

Failure to give public notice invalidated the decision.

Lord Denning
'Parliament has laid down these requirements so as to ensure that the electors can make their objections and have them properly considered. We must see that their rights are upheld.'

Agricultural, Horticultural and Forestry Industry Training Board v Aylesbury Mushroom Ltd [1972] 1 WLR 190.

HL *Ridge v Baldwin* [1964] AC 40

A chief constable was dismissed after his trial. Regulations under the Police Act 1919 required a formal inquiry before a chief constable could be dismissed.

The regulations applied to the case and hence the formal inquiry should have been heard prior to any decision to dismiss.

Lord Morris

' ... inasmuch as the decision was arrived at in complete disregard of the regulations it must be regarded as void and of no effect'.

11.4.2 Natural justice – the right to a hearing

HL *Ridge v Baldwin* [1964] AC 40

See above.

In dismissing the chief constable the defendants had not only departed from the applicable regulations but had also acted in breach of the principles of natural justice.

This case marked a change in the law. Prior to this, the rules of natural justice had been applied to only judicial and quasi-judicial decisions. In this case the House of Lords moved away from this limitation and instead focussed on the consequences of the action. If the consequences will infringe a person's rights then the rules of natural justice apply. However, certain factors may override the right to a hearing, such as, for example, national security (see the *GCHQ case*).

11.4.3 Natural justice – the duty to give reasons

HL *R v Secretary of State for the Home Department, ex parte Doody* [1993] 3 WLR 154

The Criminal Justice Act 1991 gives the Home Secretary the power to release, on the direction of the Parole Board, discretionary life prisoners after they have served a tariff period. This period is recommended by the trial judge. The prisoner was not informed of this.

The prisoner is entitled to know the length of the tariff period recommended and other relevant factors.

Lord Mustill
'The giving of reasons may be inconvenient, but I can see no grounds at all why it should be against the public interest: indeed, rather the reverse. That being so, I would ask simply: is refusal to give reasons fair? I would answer without hesitation that it is not.'

It has been argued that the scope of natural justice is in fact the requirement that powers are exercised 'fairly'.

This, according to *Doody*, demands that the context of the decision be considered. Fairness will therefore usually require that where a person will be adversely affected by the decision, they should be able to make representations and in order to do so should be informed of the reasons or nature of the case.

In *R v Secretary of State for the Home Department, ex parte Al Fayed* [1997] 1 All ER 228 the Home Secretary failed to give reasons for the refusal to grant the applicant a passport, so the decision was quashed (although after the Court of Appeal decision the Home Secretary decided to give reasons and hence Al Fayed withdrew an appeal to the House of Lords). See also *R v Director of Public Prosecutions, ex parte Manning and Another* [2000] 3 WLR 463. The concept of fairness is also linked to that of legitimate expectation (see below).

11.4.4 Natural justice – the rule against bias

HL **Dimes v Grand Junction Canal Co** (1852) 3 HL Cas 759

Lord Cottenham had adjudicated in a decision involving Grand Junction Canal Ltd but held shares in the company.

The mere existence of any financial interest in the decision will constitute bias.

Metropolitan Properties Co v Lannon [1969] 1 QB 577.

HL **R v Bow Street Magistrates' Court, ex parte Pinochet (No 2)** [1999] 2 WLR 272

Extradition proceedings against Pinochet were challenged on the basis that one of the judges, Lord Hoffmann, was an unpaid director of a charitable subsidiary of Amnesty International, which had been permitted to give evidence.

It was irrelevant that there was no actual bias; the public could reasonably believe that Lord Hoffmann was biased.

A judge is automatically disqualified where they are a member of an organisation party to the case, regardless of whether there is any financial interest.

HL | *Porter v Magill* [2002] 2 AC 357

The leader of Westminster Council was alleged to have adopted a policy of selling properties to tenants who would then vote Conservative. The auditor, Magill, was alleged to have prejudged the issue in press announcements and was therefore biased.

The test for establishing bias was whether a 'fair minded and informed observer' would conclude that there was a 'real possibility' of bias.

11.4.5 Legitimate expectation

PC | *A-G for Hong Kong v Ng Yuen Shiu* [1983] 2 AC 629

The applicant was an illegal immigrant who was threatened with deportation from Hong Kong. The Director of Immigration had publicly stated that every immigrant would be entitled to an interview before deportation and that each case would be decided on its merits.

The public statements had created a legitimate expectation and failure to then meet these expectations invalidated the decision to deport.

There can be difficulties though when policy changes; can the affected person claim that their case be decided on the basis of the previous policy? The answer seems to be that they can. For example, in *R v North and East Devon Health Authority, ex parte Coughlan* [2001] QB 213 the applicant was severely disabled and lived in a home that she had been told would be for life. The Health Authority then decided to change policy and as a result closed the home. It was held that a legitimate expectation had been created, and to decide otherwise would be unfair. In addition there was no overriding public interest to justify enforcing the new policy. This decision does raise potential problems; a court will have to carefully balance the interests of fairness given the individual's legitimate expectations against the necessity in reality for authorities to be able to change policy should it be necessary.

See also *CCSU v Minister for the Civil Service* [1985] AC 374; *R v Ministry of Agriculture, ex parte Hamble Fisheries Ltd* [1995] 2 All ER 714; and *R (Bibi) v Newham LBC* (2001) *The Times,* 10 May.

INDEX

acts *see* legislation; statutes
advertising, in elections 37
arrest
  freedom from 42
  Police and Criminal Evidence Act
    1984 96–8
assembly/association, freedom of
  100–5

bail, denial of 110
bias, rule against 145–6
Bill of Rights (1688) 3, 20–1, 43,
  54, 57–8
binding future Parliaments 19, 27–8,
  79–80, 86
Boundary Commissions/Committees
  (electoral) 34–36
breach of the peace 100, 102–5
broadcasting, in elections 39–41

campaigns, electoral 36–41
censorship *see* freedom of expression
civil liberties 89–105 *see also* human
    rights
  freedom of association/assembly
    100–5
  freedom of expression/speech 40,
    42–5, 90–6, 104–5
  freedom of person 96–9
Civil Procedure Rules (CPR) Pt.54
    123–4
civil proceedings, immunity from
  Members of Parliament 42
  Police 98–9
colonial laws, parliamentary
    supremacy 29–30
common law, supremacy of statute
    law 2, 9
communications, interception of
    111–12

compatibility
  declarations/statements of 33,
    114–19
  national law, with EC law 22,
    72–3, 80–3, 115
conditions, unreasonable 140
confidence, law of 5, 113
conflicts, legal
  convention vs. legislation 6
  fairness vs. legitimate expectation
    146–7
  freedom of expression vs. breach of
    peace 104–5
  national law vs. EC law 55, 67–8,
    84–6, 90–1
  parliamentary supremacy vs. rule
    of law 15
  validity vs. effectiveness argument
    19, 31–2
consent, to change
  constitution 30–1
  convention 6–7
considerations, relevant/irrelevant
    (judicial review) 36–7
conspiracy, to corrupt public morals
    95–6
constituency quotas 35–6
constitutional change 30–1
constitutional doctrines 9, 10–18, 79
  powers, separation of 17–18
  rule of law 10–17
constitutional statutes 3–4
  parliamentary supremacy 19, 33
construction, rule of 80–3
contempt
  of court 15–16, 93–5
  of Parliament 47–8
conventions 9
  consent to change 6–7
  enforcement of 5, 6

and judicial powers 6–8
legislation, conflicts with 6
of ministerial responsibility 49,
    50–2
and natural justice 8
non legal nature of 5
and parliamentary supremacy 7–8
corruption of public morals 95–6
courts *see* judiciary
Crichel Down Affair 51
crime, prevention of, contempt of
    court 94
criminal acts, and parliamentary
    privilege 42
criminal law, and retrospective
    legislation 14
criminals, right to vote 35

de facto power vs. *de jure* power 31
declaration of war 62–3
declarations of incompatibility 33,
    114–19
defamation 45–6
delegated legislation 30
delegation, unauthorised 137
demonstrations 101–2
deportation 108–9
direct effect, of EC law 69–72
Directives (EC), direct effect of 70–1
discretion, fettered 138
disputed elections 41

ECHR *see* European Convention on
    Human Rights
elections 34
advertising/broadcasting during
    37, 39–41
campaign conduct 36–9
disputed 41
and freedom of speech 40
judicial intervention
    during 40–1
in constituency quotas 35–6
right to vote 35
electoral law *see* elections
enforcement, of EC law 69–72, 82

'enrolled act' rule 19, 23–7, 86
entrenchment, of law 4, 29, 33, 86
error, of law/fact 133–4
European Communities Act 1972 3,
    4–5, 78–88
compatibility with national law
    (s.2) 22, 72–3, 80–3, 115
European Community law *see also*
    European Communities Act
direct application 79
direct effect 69–72
enforcement of 69–72, 82
'enrolled act' rule 86
indirect effect 72–3
and national law
    compatibility with 22, 72–3,
    80–3, 114–19
    set aside of 84–6
    supremacy over 66–8, 79–80
preliminary references to 65–6
and State liability 74–7
European Convention on Human
    Rights *see* freedom from torture
    (Art.3); freedom of expression
    (Art.10); right to fair trial
    (Art.6); right to liberty (Art.5);
    right to life (Art.2); right to
    private life (Art.8)
and Police powers 98–9
and retrospective legislation 13–15
euthanasia, voluntary 107
evidence, admissibility 115
    obtained under torture 17, 109
executive *see* Parliament
express repeal 3, 87–8
expression, freedom of 40, 42–5,
    90–6, 104–5

fair trial, right to 45, 99, 110, 115
fairness, concept of 144–7
fettered discretion 138
financial interest *see* bias
freedom from arrest 42
freedom from torture/inhuman
    treatment 99, 108–9

freedom of association/assembly
    100–1
    and breach of peace 102–5
freedom of expression/speech 40,
    42–5, 90–6, 104–5
    and breach of peace 104–5
        contempt of court 93–5
        obscenity 95–6
freedom of parliamentary
    proceedings 42–5
freedom of person 96–9
    and Police powers 98–9

GCHQ Case (1985) 131–2
Government of Wales Act 1998 4

Hansard
    and parliamentary privilege 46
    and statutory interpretation 47
highways, obstruction of 101–2
Highways Act 1986 101–2
homosexuality 95–6, 112–13
horizontal direct effect (EC law)
    69–71
House of Commons
    consent for constitutional change
        30–1
    extending powers of 30–1
    resolutions of 27
House of Lords, reducing powers of
    30–1
human rights
    civil liberties 89–105
    and contempt of court 93–4
    and elections 35
    to fair trial 45, 99, 100, 115
freedom from torture/inhuman
    treatment 99, 108–9
    to liberty 99, 109–10, 119
    to life 99, 107
    and parliamentary privilege 45
    and Police powers 99
    to private life 45, 111–13, 141
Human Rights Act 1998 3, 4, 99
    declarations of incompatibility
        (s.4) 114–17

judicial interpretation (s.3) 33,
    114–17
public authorities (s.6) 114–17, 125

illegality
    error of law/fact 133–4
    fettered discretion 138
    improper purpose 134–6
    relevant/irrelevant considerations
        136–7
    ultra vires 132
    unauthorised delegation 137
immunity
    of acts done in trade disputes
        17–18
    of Police, in civil proceedings 98–9
implied repeal 3–5, 19, 27, 28, 87–8
improper purpose 134–6
impropriety, procedural, judicial
    review 142–7
incompatibility,
    declarations/statements of 33,
    114–19
incorporation into national law,
    treaties 79–80
indirect effect, EC law 72–3
intention, parliamentary *see* statutory
    interpretation
Interception of Communications Act
    1985 111–12
international law, and Parliamentary
    powers 22–3
irrationality (judicial review) *see*
    unreasonableness

'judicial deference' 117
judicial review
    applications, procedure for 123–4
    declarations of incompatibility 118
    exclusion of 128–9
    grounds
        illegality 131–8
        irrationality/unreasonableness
            131, 139–41
        procedural impropriety 142–7
    locus standi 125–8

and prerogative powers 59–63
and private bodies 126–8
and public interest 125–8
relevant/irrelevant considerations 136–7
and rule of law 129
ultra vires 128–9
judiciary
control over Parliament 18, 23–7, 47–8
rule of law 12
and convention 6–8
and electoral constituency quotas 35–6
preliminary references to EC 65–6
statutory interpretation by 17–18, 47, 72–3, 82, 114–17
validation of statutes by 19, 23–7
juveniles, right to fair trial 110

law making *see also* legislation
judicial 17–18, 23–7
by monarch (*see* Royal Prerogative)
parliamentary 19, 20–1, 30–1
legal aid, denial of 110
legislation *see also* law making; repeal; statutes
to alter powers, of Commons/Lords 30–1
delegated 30
hierarchy of 4, 33
inconsistent 28
intention behind 13, 46–47, 90
judicial control over 17–18, 23–7
judicial interpretation of 47, 72–3, 82, 114–17
need for clarity in 12–13
powers, of Parliament to make 19, 20–1, 30–1
retrospective 2, 13–15, 21
rule of construction 80–3
vs. convention 6
legitimate expectation 146–7
liberty, right to 99, 109–10, 119
life, right to 99, 107 *see also* private life

limitations
of international law 22–3
on parliamentary supremacy 29–33
validity vs. effectiveness argument 19, 31–2
locus standi 125–8

Magna Carta (1215) 3
manner and form argument 19, 29–31
Members of Parliament *see also* Ministers
freedom from arrest 42
freedom of speech 42–5
mercy 60–1
Ministerial Code, of Conduct and Guidance on Procedure for Ministers 2001 51–2
Ministers *see also* Members
duties and accountability of 15–16, 49–52, 137
resignation of 52

national law
causal link, breach with damage 74–5
choice and form 70, 74
compatibility with EC law 22, 72–3, 80–3, 115
supremacy of EC law 66–8, 79–80, 91–2, 94
treaties, incorporation into 79–80, 90–1
national security
contempt of court 94
right to hearing 143
right to liberty 109
supremacy of EC law 91–2, 94
natural justice 143–6
and convention 8
Nicholls Committee (parliamentary privilege) 44

obscenity 95–6

obstruction
    of highway 101–2
    of Police 102–4
officials
    conduct during elections 36–7
    and rule of law 9, 10
    subject to law/courts 9, 15–16
ouster clauses 128–9

PACE *see* Police and Criminal
    Evidence Act 1984
pardons 60–1
Parliament 34–48 *see also*
    parliamentary privilege;
    parliamentary supremacy
    binding future Parliaments 19,
        27–8, 79–80, 86
    composition and procedure 47–8
    and constitutional change 30–1
    contempt of 47–8
    and criminal law 14
    de jure vs. *de facto* powers 31
    electoral law 35–41
    hierarchy of acts 4, 33
    international law, limitations of
        22–3
    judicial control over 2, 18, 23–7,
        47–8
    legislative intention of 13, 46–47,
        90
    Members of 42–5
    Ministers 15–16, 49, 50–2, 137
    retrospective legislation 14
    unconstitutional acts 8
Parliament Act 1911 6, 30
Parliament Act 1949 30
parliamentary privilege 34
    freedom from arrest 42
    freedom of speech/proceedings
        42–5
    and Hansard 46
    and human rights 45
    and judicial control 46–7
    and public interest 45
    qualified 45
    Select Committee on 43–5

parliamentary proceedings 34
    freedom of 42–5
    Select Committee on privilege
        43–5
parliamentary supremacy 2–5, 7–8,
    19
    and colonial laws 29–30
    and constitutional statutes 33
        and convention 7, 31
        and EC law 55, 79–80, 84–6
        'enrolled act' rule 19, 23–7, 86
    implied repeal 3–5, 27–8, 86
    law making powers 20–3
    limitations on 29–33
        validity vs. effectiveness
            argument 31–2
        manner and form argument 29–31
    and rule of law 15
passports, and prerogative powers
    60–1
person, freedom of 96–9
Police
    arrest, powers of 96–8, 104
    breach of peace 102–4
    and demonstrations 103
    and European Convention on
        Human Rights 98–9
    immunity from civil actions 98–9
    obstruction of 102–4
Police and Criminal Evidence Act
    1984 96–8
powers, separation of (judiciary vs.
    Parliament) 9, 17–18
preliminary references, to EC 65–6
prerogative powers
    Bill of Rights 1688 20–1
    declaration of war/deployment of
        troops 62–3
    judicial review 59–60
    modern usage of 57–8
    pardons/mercy 60–1
    passports 60–1
    and Queen's peace 57–8
    Royal prerogative 20–1, 53–4
    and treaties 60–1
    vs. statute law 55–7

pressure groups 126–7
Prevention of Terrorism (Temporary Provisions) Act 1974 109
prisoners, rights of 99
privacy *see* private life
private bodies, and judicial review 126–8
private life, right to respect for 45, 111–13, 141
privilege *see* parliamentary privilege
procedural impropriety
  judicial review 142–7
  natural justice 143–6
processions 101–2
proclamations, monarch's power to issue 20–1
proof, burden of (EC law) 75–7
proportionality 134, 139–41
public authorities/bodies 114–17, 119–21
  definition 124–5
  judicial review 123–5
public interest
  duty to give reasons 144–5
  judicial review 125–8
  parliamentary privilege 45
  supremacy of EC law 91–2, 94
Public Order Act 1986 100–1
publication, prevention of 113
punishment, and rule of law 10

qualified privilege 44–5
Queen's peace 57–8, 100, 102–5

reasons, duty to give 97–8, 144–5
Reform Acts 3
Register of Members' Interests 45
repeal, of legislation
  express 3, 87–8
  implied 3–5, 19, 27, 87–8
    inconsistent legislation 28
  parliamentary supremacy 19, 27–8
  prerogative powers 55
  retrospective 2
  statutes of constitutional significance 3–4, 28, 33, 88

Representation of the People Act 1983 37–9
resignation, of Ministers 52
resolutions, legal force of 27
retrospective legislation 2, 13–15, 21
retrospective repeal 2
right to effective remedy 45
right to fair trial 45, 99, 100, 115
right to hearing 143
right to liberty 99, 109–10, 119
right to life 99, 107
right to private life 45, 111–13, 141
Royal Prerogative 2, 20–1 *see also* prerogative powers
  curtailment of 53–4
  and statute law 55–7
  and treaties 79
rule of construction 80–3
rule of law 9, 10–17
  duty to act within 10–13
  and judicial review 129
  need for clarity 12–13
  punishment and 10
  terrorists, powers to detain 16–17
Rules of the Supreme Court (RSC) Ord.53 123–4

Scotland Act 1998 4
Select Committee, on privilege 43–5
seriousness of breach, and state liability 74–7
set aside, of conflicting national law 84–6
sexual life, privacy of 112–13, 115
sovereign rights, EC limitations on 66–8
speech, freedom of 40, 42–5, 90–6
State, definition 71–2, 75
State liability 86
  failure to implement EC law 73–4
  seriousness of breach 74–7
statute law
  common law, relationship with 2
  and Royal Prerogative 55–7
Statute of Westminster 1931 6–7
statutes 9 *see also* legislation

constitutional/of constitutional
significance 3–4, 28, 33, 88
inconsistent, implied repeal of 28
ordinary 3–5, 33, 88
repeal of 3–5, 19, 27–8, 33, 88
statutory interpretation 17–18, 72–3
and EC law 82
and Hansard 47
and Human Rights Act 1998 s.3
33, 114–17
parliamentary intention 13, 47, 90
statutory procedure, duty to follow
142–3
sufficient interest/standing (judicial
review) *see locus standi*
supremacy *see also* parliamentary
supremacy
of EC law 66–8, 84–6, 91–2, 94
Supreme Court Act 1981 s.31
(judicial review) 123–4

telephone tapping 111–12
terrorism, prevention of 109
terrorists, powers to detain 16–17,
108–10
'time of emergency' 16, 20
torture
evidence obtained under 17, 109
freedom from 99, 108–9
trade disputes, immunity of acts
under 17–18
treaties
direct effect of 69
incorporation of 79–80, 90–1
and prerogative powers 60–1, 79
repudiation of 87–8
trespassory assembly 100–1
troops, deployment of 62–3

ultra vires 128–9, 132
and prerogative powers 56
unconstitutional acts 8
unlawful assembly 100
unreasonableness 131
proportionality 140–1
unreasonable conditions 140

Wednesbury unreasonableness 139,
141

validity vs. effectiveness argument 19,
31–2
vertical direct effect 69–72
vote, right to 35

war
declaration of 62–3
War Damages Act 1956 2, 21
Wednesbury unreasonableness 139,
141